CONTENTS

AF668117

1. Guess the Number Game

```
import java.util.Scanner;
public class GuessTheNumber {
  public static void main(String[] args) {
    Scanner scanner = new Scanner(System.in);
    int secretNumber = (int) (Math.random() * 100) + 1; // Random number between 1 and 100
        int attempts = 0;
        boolean hasGuessedCorrectly = false;
        System.out.println("Welcome to Guess the Number game!");
        System.out.println("I have chosen a number between 1 and 100. Try to guess it.");
        while (!hasGuessedCorrectly) {
          System.out.print("Enter your guess: ");
          int guess = scanner.nextInt();
          attempts++;
          if (guess < secretNumber) {
            System.out.println("Too low! Try again.");
          } else if (guess > secretNumber) {
            System.out.println("Too high! Try again.");
          } else {
            System.out.println("Congratulations! You've guessed the number in " + attempts +
    " attempts.");
            hasGuessedCorrectly = true;
          }
        }
        scanner.close();
      }
    }
```

2. Rock, Paper, Scissors

```
import java.util.Scanner;
public class RockPaperScissors {
   public static void main(String[] args) {
      Scanner scanner = new Scanner(System.in);
      System.out.println("Welcome to Rock, Paper, Scissors!");
      System.out.println("Enter your move: rock, paper, or scissors.");
      System.out.print("Your move: ");
      String playerMove = scanner.nextLine().toLowerCase(); // Read player's move
      if (!isValidMove(playerMove)) {
         System.out.println("Invalid move. Please enter 'rock', 'paper', or 'scissors'.");
      } else {
         String computerMove = generateComputerMove(); // Generate computer's move
         System.out.println("Computer's move: " + computerMove);

         // Determine the winner
         String result = determineWinner(playerMove, computerMove);
         System.out.println(result);
      }
      scanner.close();
   }
   // Method to check if the player's move is valid
   public static boolean isValidMove(String move) {
      return move.equals("rock") || move.equals("paper") || move.equals("scissors");
   }
   // Method to generate the computer's move randomly
   public static String generateComputerMove() {
      int randomNum = (int) (Math.random() * 3); // Random number between 0 and 2
      switch (randomNum) {
         case 0:
            return "rock";
         case 1:
            return "paper";
```

```
        case 2:
            return "scissors";
        default:
            return ""; // This case will never occur
    }
  }
  // Method to determine the winner
  public static String determineWinner(String playerMove, String computerMove) {
    if (playerMove.equals(computerMove)) {
        return "It's a tie!";
    } else if ((playerMove.equals("rock") && computerMove.equals("scissors")) ||
            (playerMove.equals("paper") && computerMove.equals("rock")) ||
            (playerMove.equals("scissors") && computerMove.equals("paper"))) {
        return "You win!";
    } else {
        return "Computer wins!";
    }
  }
}
```

3. Dice Roll Simulator

```
import java.util.Random;
import java.util.Scanner;
public class DiceRollSimulator {
 public static void main(String[] args) {
        Scanner scanner = new Scanner(System.in);
        Random random = new Random();
        System.out.println("Welcome to the Dice Roll Simulator!");
        System.out.println("Press enter to roll the dice. Enter 'q' to quit.");

        while (true) {
          System.out.print("Roll the dice (press Enter): ");
          String input = scanner.nextLine().trim();
          if (input.equalsIgnoreCase("q")) {
            System.out.println("Thanks for playing!");
            break;
          }
          // Generate a random number between 1 and 6 (inclusive) for the dice roll
          int diceResult = random.nextInt(6) + 1;
          System.out.println("You rolled: " + diceResult);
        }
        scanner.close();
      }
   }
```

4. Hangman Game

```
import java.util.Scanner;
public class HangmanGame {
    private static final String[] WORDS = {"java", "programming", "hangman", "computer",
"science"};
    private static final int MAX_TRIES = 6;
    public static void main(String[] args) {
        Scanner scanner = new Scanner(System.in);
        String wordToGuess = selectRandomWord();
        char[] guessedLetters = new char[wordToGuess.length()];
        int remainingAttempts = MAX_TRIES;
        // Initialize guessedLetters array with underscores
        for (int i = 0; i < guessedLetters.length; i++) {
            guessedLetters[i] = '_';
        }
        System.out.println("Welcome to Hangman!");
        System.out.println("Guess the word: " + String.valueOf(guessedLetters));
        while (remainingAttempts > 0 && contains(guessedLetters, '_')) {
            System.out.println("Remaining attempts: " + remainingAttempts);
            System.out.print("Enter a letter: ");
            char guess = scanner.nextLine().toLowerCase().charAt(0);
            boolean found = false;
            for (int i = 0; i < wordToGuess.length(); i++) {
                if (wordToGuess.charAt(i) == guess) {
                    guessedLetters[i] = guess;
                    found = true;
                }
            }
            if (!found) {
                remainingAttempts--;
            }
            System.out.println("Current progress: " + String.valueOf(guessedLetters));
        }
```

```
        if (!contains(guessedLetters, '_')) {
            System.out.println("Congratulations! You guessed the word: " + wordToGuess);
        } else {
            System.out.println("Out of attempts! The word was: " + wordToGuess);
        }
        scanner.close();
    }
    private static String selectRandomWord() {
        return WORDS[(int) (Math.random() * WORDS.length)];
    }
    private static boolean contains(char[] array, char target) {
        for (char element : array) {
            if (element == target) {
                return true;
            }
        }
        return false;
    }
}
```

5. Tic-Tac-Toe

```
import java.util.Scanner;
public class TicTacToe {
   private static char[][] board = new char[3][3];
   private static char currentPlayer = 'X';
   public static void main(String[] args) {
      initializeBoard();
      displayBoard();
      Scanner scanner = new Scanner(System.in);
      boolean gameWon = false;
      while (!gameWon && !isBoardFull()) {
         System.out.println("Player " + currentPlayer + ", enter your move (row[1-3] column[1-
3]): ");
         int row = scanner.nextInt() - 1;
         int col = scanner.nextInt() - 1;
         if (isValidMove(row, col)) {
            board[row][col] = currentPlayer;
            displayBoard();
            gameWon = checkForWin(row, col);
            currentPlayer = (currentPlayer == 'X') ? 'O' : 'X';
         } else {
            System.out.println("Invalid move. Try again.");
         }
      }
      if (gameWon) {
         System.out.println("Player " + currentPlayer + " wins!");
      } else {
         System.out.println("It's a draw!");
      }
      scanner.close();
   }
   private static void initializeBoard() {
      for (int i = 0; i < 3; i++) {
```

```
        for (int j = 0; j < 3; j++) {
            board[i][j] = '-';
        }
    }
}
private static void displayBoard() {
    System.out.println("-------------");
    for (int i = 0; i < 3; i++) {
        System.out.print("| ");
        for (int j = 0; j < 3; j++) {
            System.out.print(board[i][j] + " | ");
        }
        System.out.println();
        System.out.println("-------------");
    }
}
private static boolean isValidMove(int row, int col) {
    return row >= 0 && row < 3 && col >= 0 && col < 3 && board[row][col] == '-';
}
private static boolean isBoardFull() {
    for (int i = 0; i < 3; i++) {
        for (int j = 0; j < 3; j++) {
            if (board[i][j] == '-') {
                return false;
            }
        }
    }
    return true;
}
private static boolean checkForWin(int row, int col) {
    // Check row
    if (board[row][0] == board[row][1] && board[row][1] == board[row][2]) {
        return true;
```

```
        }
        // Check column
        if (board[0][col] == board[1][col] && board[1][col] == board[2][col]) {
            return true;
        }
        // Check diagonals
        if ((row == col || row + col == 2) &&
            (board[0][0] == board[1][1] && board[1][1] == board[2][2] ||
             board[0][2] == board[1][1] && board[1][1] == board[2][0])) {
            return true;
        }
        return false;
    }
}
```

6. Memory Match Game

```
import java.util.Arrays;
import java.util.Collections;
import java.util.List;
import java.util.Scanner;
public class MemoryMatchGame {
   private static final int GRID_SIZE = 4; // Grid size (4x4 grid)
   private static final char HIDDEN_CARD = '*'; // Symbol representing a facedown card
   private static final char[] CARD_SYMBOLS = { 'A', 'B', 'C', 'D', 'E', 'F', 'G', 'H' }; // Card
symbols
   private static char[][] board = new char[GRID_SIZE][GRID_SIZE];
   private static boolean[][] revealed = new boolean[GRID_SIZE][GRID_SIZE];
   private static int matchedPairs = 0;
   public static void main(String[] args) {
      initializeBoard();
      shuffleCards();
      Scanner scanner = new Scanner(System.in);
      while (matchedPairs < GRID_SIZE * GRID_SIZE / 2) {
         displayBoard();
         System.out.println("Enter row and column of the card you want to flip (e.g., 1 2): ");
         int row1 = scanner.nextInt() - 1;
         int col1 = scanner.nextInt() - 1;
         if (!isValidPosition(row1, col1) || revealed[row1][col1]) {
            System.out.println("Invalid move. Please try again.");
            continue;
         }
        revealCard(row1, col1);
         displayBoard();
         System.out.println("Enter row and column of the second card you want to flip: ");
         int row2 = scanner.nextInt() - 1;
         int col2 = scanner.nextInt() - 1;
         if (!isValidPosition(row2, col2) || revealed[row2][col2]) {
            System.out.println("Invalid move. Please try again.");
```

```
            unrevealCard(row1, col1);
            continue;
        }
        revealCard(row2, col2);
        displayBoard();
        if (board[row1][col1] == board[row2][col2]) {
            System.out.println("Match found!");
            matchedPairs++;
        } else {
            System.out.println("No match. Cards will be flipped back.");
            unrevealCard(row1, col1);
            unrevealCard(row2, col2);
        }
    }
    System.out.println("Congratulations! You've matched all pairs!");
    scanner.close();
}
private static void initializeBoard() {
    for (char[] row : board) {
        Arrays.fill(row, HIDDEN_CARD);
    }
}
private static void shuffleCards() {
    List<Character> symbolsList = Arrays.asList(CARD_SYMBOLS);
    Collections.shuffle(symbolsList);
    int index = 0;
    for (int i = 0; i < GRID_SIZE; i++) {
        for (int j = 0; j < GRID_SIZE; j++) {
            board[i][j] = symbolsList.get(index);
            index++;
        }
    }
}
```

```
  private static void displayBoard() {
    System.out.println("-------------");
    for (char[] row : board) {
      System.out.print("| ");
      for (char card : row) {
        System.out.print(revealedCard(card) + " | ");
      }
      System.out.println();
      System.out.println("-------------");
    }
  }
  private static boolean revealedCard(char card) {
    return card != HIDDEN_CARD;
  }
  private static boolean isValidPosition(int row, int col) {
    return row >= 0 && row < GRID_SIZE && col >= 0 && col < GRID_SIZE;
  }
  private static void revealCard(int row, int col) {
    revealed[row][col] = true;
  }
  private static void unrevealCard(int row, int col) {
    revealed[row][col] = false;
  }
}
```

7. Snake Game

```
import java.util.*;
public class SnakeGame {
    private static final int GRID_SIZE = 10;
    private static final char EMPTY_CELL = '.';
    private static final char SNAKE_BODY = 'o';
    private static final char SNAKE_HEAD = '@';
    private static final char FOOD_CELL = '*';
    private static LinkedList<int[]> snake; // Stores the positions of the snake's body parts
    private static int[] foodPosition; // Stores the position of the food
    private static char[][] grid; // Represents the game grid
    private static int directionRow, directionCol; // Direction of movement (up, down, left, right)
    private static boolean gameRunning;
    public static void main(String[] args) {
        initializeGame();
        Scanner scanner = new Scanner(System.in);
        while (gameRunning) {
            displayGrid();
            System.out.print("Enter direction (W/A/S/D): ");
            String input = scanner.nextLine().toUpperCase();
            switch (input) {
                case "W":
                    if (directionRow != 1) { // Prevent moving downwards when going upwards
                        directionRow = -1;
                        directionCol = 0;
                    }
                    break;
                case "A":
                    if (directionCol != 1) { // Prevent moving right when going left
                        directionRow = 0;
                        directionCol = -1;
                    }
                    break;
```

```
            case "S":
                if (directionRow != -1) { // Prevent moving upwards when going downwards
                    directionRow = 1;
                    directionCol = 0;
                }
                break;
            case "D":
                if (directionCol != -1) { // Prevent moving left when going right
                    directionRow = 0;
                    directionCol = 1;
                }
                break;
            default:
                System.out.println("Invalid input! Use W/A/S/D.");
                continue;
        }
        moveSnake();
        if (!gameRunning) {
            displayGrid();
            System.out.println("Game over! Score: " + (snake.size() - 1));
        }
    }
    scanner.close();
}
private static void initializeGame() {
    grid = new char[GRID_SIZE][GRID_SIZE];
    snake = new LinkedList<>();
    snake.add(new int[]{GRID_SIZE / 2, GRID_SIZE / 2}); // Start with a single cell snake in
the middle
    grid[GRID_SIZE / 2][GRID_SIZE / 2] = SNAKE_HEAD;
    placeFood();
    directionRow = 0; // Initially stationary
    directionCol = 0;
```

```
        gameRunning = true;
    }
    private static void displayGrid() {
        System.out.println("Score: " + (snake.size() - 1));
        for (char[] row : grid) {
            System.out.println(Arrays.toString(row).replaceAll(",", "").replaceAll("\\[|\\]", ""));
        }
    }
    private static void moveSnake() {
        int[] head = snake.getFirst();
        int[] newHead = { head[0] + directionRow, head[1] + directionCol };

        // Check if new head hits wall or itself
        if (newHead[0] < 0 || newHead[0] >= GRID_SIZE || newHead[1] < 0 || newHead[1] >=
GRID_SIZE
                || grid[newHead[0]][newHead[1]] == SNAKE_BODY) {
            gameRunning = false;
            return;
        }
        snake.addFirst(newHead); // Move the snake
        if (Arrays.equals(newHead, foodPosition)) {
            grid[foodPosition[0]][foodPosition[1]] = EMPTY_CELL; // Remove food
            placeFood(); // Place new food
        } else {
            int[] tail = snake.removeLast();
            grid[tail[0]][tail[1]] = EMPTY_CELL; // Clear the tail
        }
        grid[newHead[0]][newHead[1]] = SNAKE_HEAD; // Update head position
        for (int[] part : snake) {
            grid[part[0]][part[1]] = SNAKE_BODY; // Update body parts
        }
    }
    private static void placeFood() {
```

```
        Random random = new Random();
        int row, col;
        do {
            row = random.nextInt(GRID_SIZE);
            col = random.nextInt(GRID_SIZE);
        } while (grid[row][col] != EMPTY_CELL);
        foodPosition = new int[]{row, col};
        grid[row][col] = FOOD_CELL;
    }
}
```

8. Pong Game

```
import java.util.Scanner;
public class PongGame {
   private static final int WIDTH = 60;
   private static final int HEIGHT = 20;
   private static final char PADDLE_CHAR = '|';
   private static final char BALL_CHAR = 'O';
   private static int paddle1Pos;
   private static int paddle2Pos;
   private static int ballX;
   private static int ballY;
   private static int ballVelX;
   private static int ballVelY;
   private static boolean gameRunning;
   public static void main(String[] args) {
      initializeGame();
      Scanner scanner = new Scanner(System.in);
      while (gameRunning) {
         displayFrame();
         updateGame();
         System.out.print("Player 1: W/S to move paddle up/down. Player 2: I/K to move paddle
up/down. Q to quit.\n");
         String input = scanner.nextLine().toUpperCase();
         if (input.equals("Q")) {
            gameRunning = false;
         } else if (input.equals("W")) {
            movePaddle1(-1); // Move paddle1 up
         } else if (input.equals("S")) {
            movePaddle1(1); // Move paddle1 down
         } else if (input.equals("I")) {
            movePaddle2(-1); // Move paddle2 up
         } else if (input.equals("K")) {
            movePaddle2(1); // Move paddle2 down
```

```
            }
        }
        scanner.close();
        System.out.println("Game over!");
    }
    private static void initializeGame() {
        paddle1Pos = HEIGHT / 2;
        paddle2Pos = HEIGHT / 2;
        ballX = WIDTH / 2;
        ballY = HEIGHT / 2;
        ballVelX = 1;
        ballVelY = 1;
        gameRunning = true;
    }
    private static void displayFrame() {
        for (int y = 0; y < HEIGHT; y++) {
            for (int x = 0; x < WIDTH; x++) {
                if (x == 0 || x == WIDTH - 1) {
                    System.out.print("#"); // Draw side walls
                } else if (x == 1 && y == paddle1Pos || x == WIDTH - 2 && y == paddle2Pos) {
                    System.out.print(PADDLE_CHAR); // Draw paddles
                } else if (x == ballX && y == ballY) {
                    System.out.print(BALL_CHAR); // Draw ball
                } else {
                    System.out.print(" "); // Empty space
                }
            }
            System.out.println();
        }
    }
    private static void updateGame() {
        // Move the ball
        ballX += ballVelX;
```

```
        ballY += ballVelY;
        // Check collision with top/bottom walls
        if (ballY == 0 || ballY == HEIGHT - 1) {
            ballVelY = -ballVelY;
        }
        // Check collision with paddles
        if (ballX == 2 && ballY == paddle1Pos || ballX == WIDTH - 3 && ballY == paddle2Pos)
{
            ballVelX = -ballVelX;
        }
        // Check if ball goes out of bounds
        if (ballX == 0 || ballX == WIDTH - 1) {
            gameRunning = false;
        }
    }
    private static void movePaddle1(int dir) {
        paddle1Pos = Math.max(0, Math.min(HEIGHT - 1, paddle1Pos + dir));
    }
    private static void movePaddle2(int dir) {
        paddle2Pos = Math.max(0, Math.min(HEIGHT - 1, paddle2Pos + dir));
    }
}
```

9. Brick Breaker Game

```
import java.util.*;
public class BrickBreakerGame {
    private static final int WIDTH = 20;
    private static final int HEIGHT = 10;
    private static final char PADDLE_CHAR = '=';
    private static final char BALL_CHAR = 'O';
    private static final char BRICK_CHAR = '#';
    private static char[][] grid;
    private static int paddlePos;
    private static int ballX, ballY;
    private static int ballVelX, ballVelY;
    private static boolean gameRunning;
    public static void main(String[] args) {
        initializeGame();
        Scanner scanner = new Scanner(System.in);
        while (gameRunning) {
            displayGrid();
            updateGame();
            System.out.print("Move paddle (A/D): ");
            String input = scanner.nextLine().toUpperCase();
            switch (input) {
                case "A":
                    movePaddle(-1); // Move paddle left
                    break;
                case "D":
                    movePaddle(1); // Move paddle right
                    break;
                default:
                    System.out.println("Invalid input! Use A or D.");
                    break;
            }
        }
```

```
        scanner.close();
        System.out.println("Game over!");
    }
    private static void initializeGame() {
        grid = new char[HEIGHT][WIDTH];
        paddlePos = WIDTH / 2;
        ballX = WIDTH / 2;
        ballY = HEIGHT - 2;
        ballVelX = 1;
        ballVelY = -1;
        gameRunning = true;
        // Initialize grid with bricks
        for (int i = 0; i < HEIGHT - 3; i++) {
            for (int j = 0; j < WIDTH; j++) {
                grid[i][j] = BRICK_CHAR;
            }
        }
    }
    private static void displayGrid() {
        for (char[] row : grid) {
            for (char cell : row) {
                System.out.print(cell);
            }
            System.out.println();
        }
        // Display paddle and ball
        for (int i = 0; i < WIDTH; i++) {
            if (i == paddlePos) {
                System.out.print(PADDLE_CHAR);
            } else if (i == ballX && ballY >= 0 && ballY < HEIGHT) {
                System.out.print(BALL_CHAR);
            } else {
                System.out.print(' ');
```

```
            }
        }
        System.out.println();
    }
    private static void updateGame() {
        // Move the ball
        ballX += ballVelX;
        ballY += ballVelY;
        // Check collision with walls and paddle
        if (ballX == 0 || ballX == WIDTH - 1) {
            ballVelX = -ballVelX;
        }
        if (ballY == 0) {
            ballVelY = -ballVelY;
        } else if (ballY == HEIGHT - 1) {
            if (ballX == paddlePos) {
                ballVelY = -ballVelY;
            } else {
                gameRunning = false;
            }
        }
        // Check collision with bricks
        if (ballY >= 0 && ballY < HEIGHT - 3 && grid[ballY][ballX] == BRICK_CHAR) {
            grid[ballY][ballX] = ' '; // Clear the brick
            ballVelY = -ballVelY; // Reverse ball's vertical velocity
        }
    }
    private static void movePaddle(int dir) {
        paddlePos = Math.max(0, Math.min(WIDTH - 1, paddlePos + dir));
    }
}
```

10. Simple Platformer

```
import java.util.*;
public class SimplePlatformer {
    private static final int WIDTH = 20;
    private static final int HEIGHT = 10;
    private static final char PLAYER_CHAR = 'P';
    private static final char PLATFORM_CHAR = '#';
    private static char[][] grid;
    private static int playerX;
    private static int playerY;
    private static boolean isJumping;
    private static boolean gameRunning;
    public static void main(String[] args) {
        initializeGame();
        Scanner scanner = new Scanner(System.in);
        while (gameRunning) {
            displayGrid();
            updateGame();
            System.out.print("Move (A/D to walk, W to jump, Q to quit): ");
            String input = scanner.nextLine().toUpperCase();
            switch (input) {
                case "A":
                    movePlayer(-1); // Move left
                    break;
                case "D":
                    movePlayer(1); // Move right
                    break;
                case "W":
                    jump();
                    break;
                case "Q":
                    gameRunning = false;
                    break;
```

```
            default:
                System.out.println("Invalid input! Use A/D/W/Q.");
                break;
        }
    }
    scanner.close();
    System.out.println("Game over!");
}
private static void initializeGame() {
    grid = new char[HEIGHT][WIDTH];
    playerX = WIDTH / 2;
    playerY = HEIGHT - 2;
    isJumping = false;
    gameRunning = true;
    // Build the platform-filled world
    for (int y = HEIGHT - 3; y < HEIGHT; y++) {
        for (int x = 0; x < WIDTH; x++) {
            grid[y][x] = PLATFORM_CHAR;
        }
    }
}
private static void displayGrid() {
    for (char[] row : grid) {
        for (char cell : row) {
            if (playerY >= 0 && playerY < HEIGHT && cell == PLATFORM_CHAR &&
playerX == Arrays.asList(row).indexOf(cell)) {
                System.out.print(PLAYER_CHAR); // Draw player on platform
            } else {
                System.out.print(cell); // Draw platform
            }
        }
        System.out.println();
    }
```

```
    }

    private static void updateGame() {
        if (isJumping) {
            playerY--; // Move player upward (simulate jump)
            if (playerY <= 0) {
                isJumping = false; // Reached top, start falling down
            }
        } else {
            // Check if player is standing on a platform
            if (playerY < HEIGHT - 1 && grid[playerY + 1][playerX] == PLATFORM_CHAR) {
                // Player is on a platform, do nothing
            } else {
                playerY++; // Player is falling down
            }
        }
    }
    private static void movePlayer(int dir) {
        int newX = playerX + dir;
        if (newX >= 0 && newX < WIDTH) {
            playerX = newX;
        }
    }
    private static void jump() {
        if (!isJumping && playerY >= 0 && playerY < HEIGHT - 1 && grid[playerY +
1][playerX] == PLATFORM_CHAR) {
            isJumping = true; // Start jumping only if player is on a platform
        }
    }
}
```

11. Reaction Time Tester

```
import java.util.Random;
import java.util.Scanner;
public class ReactionTimeTester {
  public static void main(String[] args) {
    Scanner scanner = new Scanner(System.in);
    Random random = new Random();
    System.out.println("Welcome to the Reaction Time Tester!");
    System.out.println("Press Enter to start the test. When you see 'GO!', press Enter again.");
    while (true) {
      System.out.println("Press Enter to begin...");
      scanner.nextLine(); // Wait for user to press Enter to start
      System.out.println("Get ready...");
      try {
        Thread.sleep(2000); // Wait for 2 seconds before displaying 'GO!'
      } catch (InterruptedException e) {
        e.printStackTrace();
      }
      System.out.println("GO!");
      long startTime = System.currentTimeMillis(); // Record the start time
      scanner.nextLine(); // Wait for user to press Enter after seeing 'GO!'
      long endTime = System.currentTimeMillis(); // Record the end time
      long reactionTime = endTime - startTime;
      System.out.println("Your reaction time: " + reactionTime + " milliseconds");
      System.out.println("Do you want to try again? (yes/no)");
      String input = scanner.nextLine().toLowerCase();
      if (!input.equals("yes")) {
        break; // End the game if user does not want to try again
      }
    }
    System.out.println("Thanks for playing the Reaction Time Tester!");
    scanner.close();
  }}
```

12. Whack-a-Mole Game

```
import java.util.*;
public class WhackAMoleGame {
    private static final int GRID_SIZE = 4;
    private static final char EMPTY_CELL = '-';
    private static final char MOLE_CHAR = 'M';
    private static char[][] grid;
    private static int score;
    private static boolean gameRunning;
    private static Random random = new Random();
    public static void main(String[] args) {
        initializeGame();
        Scanner scanner = new Scanner(System.in);
        while (gameRunning) {
            displayGrid();
            System.out.println("Enter row and column to whack (1-" + GRID_SIZE + "): ");
            int row = scanner.nextInt() - 1;
            int col = scanner.nextInt() - 1;
            if (isValidPosition(row, col)) {
                if (grid[row][col] == MOLE_CHAR) {
                    System.out.println("You whacked a mole!");
                    score++;
                } else {
                    System.out.println("Missed!");
                }
                updateGrid();
            } else {
                System.out.println("Invalid position. Please try again.");
            }
            if (score >= 10) {
                System.out.println("Congratulations! You whacked 10 moles. Game over!");
                gameRunning = false;
            }
```

```
        }
        scanner.close();
    }
    private static void initializeGame() {
        grid = new char[GRID_SIZE][GRID_SIZE];
        score = 0;
        gameRunning = true;
        // Fill the grid with empty cells
        for (char[] row : grid) {
            Arrays.fill(row, EMPTY_CELL);
        }
    }
    private static void displayGrid() {
        System.out.println("Score: " + score);
        for (char[] row : grid) {
            for (char cell : row) {
                System.out.print(cell + " ");
            }
            System.out.println();
        }
    }
    private static boolean isValidPosition(int row, int col) {
        return row >= 0 && row < GRID_SIZE && col >= 0 && col < GRID_SIZE;
    }
    private static void updateGrid() {
        // Place a mole in a random empty cell
        int randomRow = random.nextInt(GRID_SIZE);
        int randomCol = random.nextInt(GRID_SIZE);
        if (grid[randomRow][randomCol] == EMPTY_CELL) {
            grid[randomRow][randomCol] = MOLE_CHAR;
        }
        // Remove the old mole from the grid
        for (int i = 0; i < GRID_SIZE; i++) {
```

```
        for (int j = 0; j < GRID_SIZE; j++) {
          if (grid[i][j] == MOLE_CHAR) {
            grid[i][j] = EMPTY_CELL;
          }
        }
      }
    }
}
```

13. Number Matching Game

```
import java.util.*;
public class NumberMatchingGame {
   private static final int BOARD_SIZE = 4; // Assuming a 4x4 board
   private static final int NUM_PAIRS = 8; // Total number of number pairs
   private static int[][] board; // The game board
   private static int[][] displayBoard; // Displayed board (with tiles hidden)
   private static Set<Integer> hiddenNumbers; // Set to store hidden numbers
   private static int numPairsFound; // Number of pairs found by the player
   private static boolean gameRunning;
   private static Scanner scanner = new Scanner(System.in);
   public static void main(String[] args) {
      initializeGame();
      displayBoard();
      while (gameRunning) {
         int firstRow, firstCol, secondRow, secondCol;
         // Get input for the first tile
         System.out.println("Enter row and column for the first tile (0-" + (BOARD_SIZE - 1) +
"): ");
         firstRow = scanner.nextInt();
         firstCol = scanner.nextInt();
         if (!isValidInput(firstRow, firstCol) || displayBoard[firstRow][firstCol] != -1) {
            System.out.println("Invalid selection. Please try again.");
            continue;
         }
         displayBoard[firstRow][firstCol] = board[firstRow][firstCol];
         displayBoard();
         // Get input for the second tile
         System.out.println("Enter row and column for the second tile (0-" + (BOARD_SIZE - 1)
+ "): ");
         secondRow = scanner.nextInt();
         secondCol = scanner.nextInt();
```

```
        if (!isValidInput(secondRow, secondCol) || displayBoard[secondRow][secondCol] != -1)
{
            System.out.println("Invalid selection. Please try again.");
            displayBoard[firstRow][firstCol] = -1; // Hide the first tile again
            continue;
        }
        displayBoard[secondRow][secondCol] = board[secondRow][secondCol];
        displayBoard();
        // Check if tiles match
        if (board[firstRow][firstCol] == board[secondRow][secondCol]) {
            System.out.println("Match found!");
            numPairsFound++;
            if (numPairsFound == NUM_PAIRS) {
                System.out.println("Congratulations! You found all pairs. Game over!");
                gameRunning = false;
            }
        } else {
            System.out.println("No match. Try again.");
            displayBoard[firstRow][firstCol] = -1; // Hide the first tile
            displayBoard[secondRow][secondCol] = -1; // Hide the second tile
        }
    }
    scanner.close();
}
private static void initializeGame() {
    // Initialize the game board and display board
    board = new int[BOARD_SIZE][BOARD_SIZE];
    displayBoard = new int[BOARD_SIZE][BOARD_SIZE];
    hiddenNumbers = new HashSet<>();
    numPairsFound = 0;
    gameRunning = true;
    // Fill the board with number pairs
    List<Integer> numbers = new ArrayList<>();
```

```
        for (int num = 1; num <= NUM_PAIRS; num++) {
            numbers.add(num);
            numbers.add(num); // Each number pair consists of two identical numbers
        }
        Collections.shuffle(numbers);
        Iterator<Integer> iterator = numbers.iterator();
        for (int i = 0; i < BOARD_SIZE; i++) {
            for (int j = 0; j < BOARD_SIZE; j++) {
                board[i][j] = iterator.next();
                displayBoard[i][j] = -1; // Hide all tiles (-1 indicates hidden)
            }
        }
    }
    private static void displayBoard() {
        System.out.println("Number Matching Game:");
        System.out.println("Pairs found: " + numPairsFound);
        for (int[] row : displayBoard) {
            for (int value : row) {
                if (value == -1) {
                    System.out.print("# "); // Hidden tile
                } else {
                    System.out.print(value + " "); // Displayed number
                }
            }
            System.out.println();
        }
    }
    private static boolean isValidInput(int row, int col) {
        return row >= 0 && row < BOARD_SIZE && col >= 0 && col < BOARD_SIZE;
    }
}
```

14. Card War Game

```
import java.util.*;
public class CardWarGame {
    private static final int NUM_CARDS = 52;
    private static final int NUM_RANKS = 13;
    private static final int NUM_SUITS = 4;
    private static final String[] RANKS = {"2", "3", "4", "5", "6", "7", "8", "9", "10", "J", "Q",
"K", "A"};
    private static final String[] SUITS = {"Hearts", "Diamonds", "Clubs", "Spades"};
    private static List<String> deck;
    private static List<String> player1Hand;
    private static List<String> player2Hand;
    private static Random random = new Random();
    public static void main(String[] args) {
        initializeGame();
        shuffleDeck();
        // Deal cards to players
        player1Hand = new ArrayList<>();
        player2Hand = new ArrayList<>();
        dealCards();
        // Play the game
        Scanner scanner = new Scanner(System.in);
        while (!player1Hand.isEmpty() && !player2Hand.isEmpty()) {
            String card1 = player1Hand.remove(0);
            String card2 = player2Hand.remove(0);
            System.out.println("Player 1 plays: " + card1);
            System.out.println("Player 2 plays: " + card2);
            int rank1 = getCardRank(card1);
            int rank2 = getCardRank(card2);
            if (rank1 > rank2) {
                System.out.println("Player 1 wins the round!");
                player1Hand.add(card1);
                player1Hand.add(card2);
```

```
        } else if (rank2 > rank1) {
            System.out.println("Player 2 wins the round!");
            player2Hand.add(card1);
            player2Hand.add(card2);
        } else {
            System.out.println("It's a tie! Cards go to the discard pile.");
        }
        System.out.println("Press Enter to continue...");
        scanner.nextLine();
    }
    scanner.close();
    // Determine the winner
    if (player1Hand.isEmpty()) {
        System.out.println("Player 2 wins the game!");
    } else {
        System.out.println("Player 1 wins the game!");
    }
}
private static void initializeGame() {
    deck = new ArrayList<>();
    for (String suit : SUITS) {
        for (String rank : RANKS) {
            deck.add(rank + " of " + suit);
        }
    }
}
private static void shuffleDeck() {
    Collections.shuffle(deck);
}
private static void dealCards() {
    for (int i = 0; i < NUM_CARDS / 2; i++) {
        player1Hand.add(deck.get(i));
        player2Hand.add(deck.get(i + NUM_CARDS / 2));
```

```
        }
    }
    private static int getCardRank(String card) {
        String rankString = card.split(" ")[0];
        for (int i = 0; i < NUM_RANKS; i++) {
            if (RANKS[i].equals(rankString)) {
                return i;
            }
        }
        return -1; // Invalid card
    }
}
```

15. Simple RPG Battle

```
import java.util.*;
public class SimpleRpgBattle {
    private static final Random random = new Random();
    private static final Scanner scanner = new Scanner(System.in);
    private static int playerHealth = 100;
    private static int enemyHealth = 50;
    private static boolean playerTurn = true;
    private static boolean gameOver = false;
    public static void main(String[] args) {
        System.out.println("Welcome to Simple RPG Battle!");
        System.out.println("You encounter an enemy. Let the battle begin!");
        while (!gameOver) {
            if (playerTurn) {
                playerTurn();
            } else {
                enemyTurn();
            }
            if (playerHealth <= 0) {
                System.out.println("You have been defeated. Game over!");
                gameOver = true;
            } else if (enemyHealth <= 0) {
                System.out.println("You defeated the enemy! Congratulations!");
                gameOver = true;
            } else {
                // Switch turns
                playerTurn = !playerTurn;
            }
        }
        scanner.close();
    }
    private static void playerTurn() {
        System.out.println("Player's turn. Choose an action:");
```

```
        System.out.println("1. Attack");
        System.out.println("2. Heal");
        int choice = getPlayerChoice();
        switch (choice) {
            case 1:
                int playerDamage = random.nextInt(10) + 10; // Random damage between 10 to 19
                System.out.println("You attack the enemy for " + playerDamage + " damage!");
                enemyHealth -= playerDamage;
                break;
            case 2:
                int healAmount = random.nextInt(10) + 10; // Random heal between 10 to 19
                System.out.println("You heal yourself for " + healAmount + " health points.");
                playerHealth = Math.min(100, playerHealth + healAmount); // Cap health at 100
                break;
            default:
                System.out.println("Invalid choice. Try again.");
                playerTurn();
                break;
        }
    }
    private static void enemyTurn() {
        System.out.println("Enemy's turn.");
        int enemyDamage = random.nextInt(5) + 5; // Random damage between 5 to 9
        System.out.println("The enemy attacks you for " + enemyDamage + " damage!");
        playerHealth -= enemyDamage;
    }
    private static int getPlayerChoice() {
        while (true) {
            try {
                System.out.print("Enter your choice: ");
                int choice = scanner.nextInt();
                if (choice < 1 || choice > 2) {
                    throw new InputMismatchException();
```

```
            }
            return choice;
        } catch (InputMismatchException e) {
            System.out.println("Invalid input. Please enter a valid choice (1 or 2).");
            scanner.nextLine(); // Clear the invalid input
        }
      }
   }
}
```

16. Connect Four Game

```
import java.util.*;
public class ConnectFourGame {
    private static final int ROWS = 6;
    private static final int COLS = 7;
    private static final char EMPTY_SLOT = '-';
    private static final char PLAYER1_PIECE = 'X';
    private static final char PLAYER2_PIECE = 'O';
    private static char[][] board;
    private static boolean player1Turn = true;
    private static boolean gameRunning = true;
    private static Scanner scanner = new Scanner(System.in);
    public static void main(String[] args) {
        initializeBoard();
        displayBoard();
        while (gameRunning) {
            int column = getColumnChoice();
            dropPiece(column);
            if (checkWin()) {
                displayBoard();
                char winnerPiece = player1Turn ? PLAYER1_PIECE : PLAYER2_PIECE;
                System.out.println("Player " + winnerPiece + " wins!");
                gameRunning = false;
            } else if (isBoardFull()) {
                displayBoard();
                System.out.println("It's a draw! The board is full.");
                gameRunning = false;
            } else {
                player1Turn = !player1Turn; // Switch turns
                displayBoard();
            }
        }
        scanner.close();
```

```
    }
    private static void initializeBoard() {
        board = new char[ROWS][COLS];
        for (int row = 0; row < ROWS; row++) {
            Arrays.fill(board[row], EMPTY_SLOT);
        }
    }
    private static void displayBoard() {
        System.out.println("  1 2 3 4 5 6 7");
        for (int row = 0; row < ROWS; row++) {
            System.out.print("|");
            for (int col = 0; col < COLS; col++) {
                System.out.print(board[row][col] + "|");
            }
            System.out.println();
        }
        System.out.println("---------------");
    }
    private static int getColumnChoice() {
        char piece = player1Turn ? PLAYER1_PIECE : PLAYER2_PIECE;
        int column;
        while (true) {
            System.out.println("Player " + piece + ", enter column (1-7): ");
            if (scanner.hasNextInt()) {
                column = scanner.nextInt();
                if (column >= 1 && column <= COLS && board[0][column - 1] == EMPTY_SLOT)
{
                    break;
                }
            }
            System.out.println("Invalid column. Please try again.");
            scanner.nextLine(); // Consume invalid input
        }
```

```
        return column - 1; // Convert to zero-based index
    }
    private static void dropPiece(int column) {
        char piece = player1Turn ? PLAYER1_PIECE : PLAYER2_PIECE;
        for (int row = ROWS - 1; row >= 0; row--) {
            if (board[row][column] == EMPTY_SLOT) {
                board[row][column] = piece;
                break;
            }
        }
    }
    private static boolean checkWin() {
        char piece = player1Turn ? PLAYER1_PIECE : PLAYER2_PIECE;
        // Check horizontal
        for (int row = 0; row < ROWS; row++) {
            for (int col = 0; col <= COLS - 4; col++) {
                if (board[row][col] == piece &&
                    board[row][col + 1] == piece &&
                    board[row][col + 2] == piece &&
                    board[row][col + 3] == piece) {
                    return true;
                }
            }
        }
        // Check vertical
        for (int row = 0; row <= ROWS - 4; row++) {
            for (int col = 0; col < COLS; col++) {
                if (board[row][col] == piece &&
                    board[row + 1][col] == piece &&
                    board[row + 2][col] == piece &&
                    board[row + 3][col] == piece) {
                    return true;
```

```
            }
        }
    }
    // Check diagonal (down-right)
    for (int row = 0; row <= ROWS - 4; row++) {
        for (int col = 0; col <= COLS - 4; col++) {
            if (board[row][col] == piece &&
                board[row + 1][col + 1] == piece &&
                board[row + 2][col + 2] == piece &&
                board[row + 3][col + 3] == piece) {
                return true;
            }
        }
    }
    // Check diagonal (up-right)
    for (int row = 3; row < ROWS; row++) {
        for (int col = 0; col <= COLS - 4; col++) {
            if (board[row][col] == piece &&
                board[row - 1][col + 1] == piece &&
                board[row - 2][col + 2] == piece &&
                board[row - 3][col + 3] == piece) {
                return true;
            }
        }
    }
    return false;
}
private static boolean isBoardFull() {
    for (int col = 0; col < COLS; col++) {
        if (board[0][col] == EMPTY_SLOT) {
            return false;
        }
    }
```

```
        return true;
    }
}
```

17. Battleship Game

```
import java.util.*;
public class BattleshipGame {
    private static final int BOARD_SIZE = 10;
    private static final char EMPTY_CELL = '-';
    private static final char SHIP_CELL = 'S';
    private static final char HIT_CELL = 'X';
    private static final char MISS_CELL = 'O';
    private static char[][] player1Board;
    private static char[][] player2Board;
    private static Scanner scanner = new Scanner(System.in);
    public static void main(String[] args) {
        System.out.println("Welcome to Battleship Game!");
        // Initialize game boards for both players
        player1Board = initializeBoard();
        player2Board = initializeBoard();
        // Place ships for both players
        placeShips(player1Board, "Player 1");
        placeShips(player2Board, "Player 2");
        // Play the game
        boolean player1Turn = true;
        boolean gameOver = false;
        while (!gameOver) {
            displayBoards(player1Board, player2Board);
            char[][] currentBoard = player1Turn ? player2Board : player1Board;
            String playerName = player1Turn ? "Player 1" : "Player 2";
            System.out.println(playerName + ", take your shot!");
            boolean validShot = false;
            while (!validShot) {
                int[] target = getTarget();
                int row = target[0];
                int col = target[1];
```

```
            if (currentBoard[row][col] == EMPTY_CELL || currentBoard[row][col] ==
SHIP_CELL) {
                validShot = true;
                if (currentBoard[row][col] == SHIP_CELL) {
                    System.out.println("It's a HIT!");
                    currentBoard[row][col] = HIT_CELL;
                    if (isGameOver(currentBoard)) {
                        displayBoards(player1Board, player2Board);
                        System.out.println(playerName + " wins!");
                        gameOver = true;
                    }
                } else {
                    System.out.println("It's a MISS!");
                    currentBoard[row][col] = MISS_CELL;
                }
            } else {
                System.out.println("Invalid target. Try again.");
            }
        }
        player1Turn = !player1Turn; // Switch turns
    }
    scanner.close();
}
private static char[][] initializeBoard() {
    char[][] board = new char[BOARD_SIZE][BOARD_SIZE];
    for (char[] row : board) {
        Arrays.fill(row, EMPTY_CELL);
    }
    return board;
}
private static void displayBoards(char[][] player1Board, char[][] player2Board) {
    System.out.println("Player 1's Board            Player 2's Board");
    for (int i = 0; i < BOARD_SIZE; i++) {
```

```
        for (int j = 0; j < BOARD_SIZE; j++) {
            System.out.print(player1Board[i][j] + " ");
        }
        System.out.print("        ");
        for (int j = 0; j < BOARD_SIZE; j++) {
            System.out.print(player2Board[i][j] + " ");
        }
        System.out.println();
    }
    System.out.println("--------------------------------------------");
}
private static void placeShips(char[][] board, String playerName) {
    System.out.println(playerName + ", place your ships!");
    int numShips = 5; // Each player places 5 ships
    while (numShips > 0) {
        System.out.println("Enter coordinates for ship " + (6 - numShips) + " (row and column,
e.g., 1 2): ");
        int[] coordinates = getTarget();
        int row = coordinates[0];
        int col = coordinates[1];
        if (board[row][col] == EMPTY_CELL) {
            board[row][col] = SHIP_CELL;
            numShips--;
        } else {
            System.out.println("Invalid placement. Cell already occupied. Try again.");
        }
    }
}
private static int[] getTarget() {
    int[] target = new int[2];
    while (true) {
        try {
            System.out.print("Row (1-10): ");
```

```
            target[0] = scanner.nextInt() - 1;
            System.out.print("Column (1-10): ");
            target[1] = scanner.nextInt() - 1;
            if (target[0] >= 0 && target[0] < BOARD_SIZE && target[1] >= 0 && target[1] <
BOARD_SIZE) {
                break;
            } else {
                System.out.println("Invalid coordinates. Please enter values between 1 and 10.");
            }
        } catch (InputMismatchException e) {
            System.out.println("Invalid input. Please enter numeric values.");
            scanner.nextLine(); // Consume invalid input
        }
    }
    return target;
  }
  private static boolean isGameOver(char[][] board) {
    for (char[] row : board) {
        for (char cell : row) {
            if (cell == SHIP_CELL) {
                return false;
            }
        }
    }
    return true;
  }
}
```

18. Simple Blackjack

```
import java.util.*;
public class SimpleBlackjack {
    private static final List<String> ranks = Arrays.asList(
            "2", "3", "4", "5", "6", "7", "8", "9", "10", "J", "Q", "K", "A"
    );
    private static final List<Integer> values = Arrays.asList(
            2, 3, 4, 5, 6, 7, 8, 9, 10, 10, 10, 10, 11
    );
    private static final Scanner scanner = new Scanner(System.in);
    private static List<String> deck;
    private static int playerScore;
    private static int dealerScore;
    public static void main(String[] args) {
        System.out.println("Welcome to Simple Blackjack!");
        while (true) {
            initializeGame();
            playRound();
            System.out.println("Do you want to play again? (yes/no)");
            String choice = scanner.nextLine().toLowerCase();
            if (!choice.equals("yes")) {
                break;
            }
        }
        System.out.println("Thanks for playing!");
        scanner.close();
    }
    private static void initializeGame() {
        deck = new ArrayList<>(ranks);
        Collections.shuffle(deck);
        playerScore = 0;
        dealerScore = 0;
    }
```

```
private static void playRound() {
    System.out.println("\nDealing cards...");
    // Initial deal
    playerScore = dealCard("Player");
    dealerScore = dealCard("Dealer");
    playerScore += dealCard("Player");
    dealerScore += dealCard("Dealer");
    // Player's turn
    while (true) {
        System.out.println("Your current score: " + playerScore);
        System.out.print("Do you want to hit or stand? (hit/stand): ");
        String choice = scanner.nextLine().toLowerCase();
        if (choice.equals("hit")) {
            playerScore += dealCard("Player");
            if (playerScore > 21) {
                System.out.println("Busted! You lose.");
                return;
            }
        } else if (choice.equals("stand")) {
            break;
        } else {
            System.out.println("Invalid input. Please try again.");
        }
    }
    // Dealer's turn
    System.out.println("\nDealer's turn...");
    while (dealerScore < 17) {
        dealerScore += dealCard("Dealer");
        System.out.println("Dealer's current score: " + dealerScore);
    }
    // Determine the winner
    determineWinner();
}
```

```
    private static int dealCard(String player) {
        String card = deck.remove(0);
        System.out.println(player + " draws: " + card);
        int index = ranks.indexOf(card);
        return values.get(index);
    }
    private static void determineWinner() {
        System.out.println("\nFinal scores:");
        System.out.println("Player: " + playerScore);
        System.out.println("Dealer: " + dealerScore);
        if (playerScore > 21) {
            System.out.println("Busted! You lose.");
        } else if (dealerScore > 21 || playerScore > dealerScore) {
            System.out.println("Congratulations! You win!");
        } else if (playerScore < dealerScore) {
            System.out.println("Dealer wins.");
        } else {
            System.out.println("It's a tie!");
        }
    }
}
```

19. Space Invaders (Text-based)

```
import java.util.*;
public class SpaceInvaders {
    private static final int ROWS = 10;
    private static final int COLS = 10;
    private static final char PLAYER_CHAR = '^';
    private static final char INVADER_CHAR = 'V';
    private static final char EMPTY_CHAR = '.';
    private static final char BULLET_CHAR = '|';
    private static char[][] grid;
    private static int playerPos;
    private static int invaderPos;
    private static boolean invaderMovingRight;
    private static boolean isGameOver;
    private static Random random = new Random();
    private static Scanner scanner = new Scanner(System.in);
    public static void main(String[] args) {
        System.out.println("Welcome to Text-based Space Invaders!");
        initializeGame();
        while (!isGameOver) {
            displayGrid();
            handlePlayerInput();
            moveInvader();
            checkCollision();
            if (isGameOver) {
                System.out.println("Game Over! Invader reached the player.");
            }
        }
        scanner.close();
    }
    private static void initializeGame() {
        grid = new char[ROWS][COLS];
        playerPos = COLS / 2;
```

```
        invaderPos = random.nextInt(COLS);
        invaderMovingRight = true;
        isGameOver = false;
        for (int row = 0; row < ROWS; row++) {
            Arrays.fill(grid[row], EMPTY_CHAR);
        }
        grid[ROWS - 1][playerPos] = PLAYER_CHAR;
        grid[0][invaderPos] = INVADER_CHAR;
    }
    private static void displayGrid() {
        for (int row = 0; row < ROWS; row++) {
            for (int col = 0; col < COLS; col++) {
                System.out.print(grid[row][col] + " ");
            }
            System.out.println();
        }
        System.out.println();
    }
    private static void handlePlayerInput() {
        System.out.print("Enter 'L' to move left, 'R' to move right, or 'F' to fire: ");
        String input = scanner.nextLine().toUpperCase();
        if (input.equals("L") && playerPos > 0) {
            grid[ROWS - 1][playerPos] = EMPTY_CHAR;
            playerPos--;
            grid[ROWS - 1][playerPos] = PLAYER_CHAR;
        } else if (input.equals("R") && playerPos < COLS - 1) {
            grid[ROWS - 1][playerPos] = EMPTY_CHAR;
            playerPos++;
            grid[ROWS - 1][playerPos] = PLAYER_CHAR;
        } else if (input.equals("F")) {
            grid[ROWS - 2][playerPos] = BULLET_CHAR;
        }
    }
```

```
    private static void moveInvader() {
        grid[0][invaderPos] = EMPTY_CHAR;
        if (invaderMovingRight) {
            if (invaderPos < COLS - 1) {
                invaderPos++;
            } else {
                invaderMovingRight = false;
                invaderPos--;
            }
        } else {
            if (invaderPos > 0) {
                invaderPos--;
            } else {
                invaderMovingRight = true;
                invaderPos++;
            }
        }
        grid[0][invaderPos] = INVADER_CHAR;
    }
    private static void checkCollision() {
        if (grid[ROWS - 2][playerPos] == BULLET_CHAR && grid[0][playerPos] ==
INVADER_CHAR) {
            isGameOver = true;
        }
    }
}
```

20. Trivia Quiz Game

```
import java.util.*;
public class TriviaQuizGame {
   private static final Scanner scanner = new Scanner(System.in);
   private static List<String> questions = new ArrayList<>();
   private static Map<String, String> answers = new HashMap<>();
   private static int score = 0;
   public static void main(String[] args) {
      initializeQuestions();
      displayWelcomeMessage();
      for (String question : questions) {
         displayQuestion(question);
         String userAnswer = getUserAnswer();
         if (checkAnswer(question, userAnswer)) {
            System.out.println("Correct!\n");
            score++;
         } else {
            System.out.println("Incorrect!\n");
         }
      }
      displayFinalScore();
      scanner.close();
   }
   private static void initializeQuestions() {
      questions.add("What is the capital of France?");
      answers.put("What is the capital of France?", "Paris");
      questions.add("Who painted the Mona Lisa?");
      answers.put("Who painted the Mona Lisa?", "Leonardo da Vinci");
      questions.add("What is the largest planet in our solar system?");
      answers.put("What is the largest planet in our solar system?", "Jupiter");
   }
   private static void displayWelcomeMessage() {
      System.out.println("Welcome to the Trivia Quiz Game!");
```

```
        System.out.println("Answer the following questions.\n");
    }
    private static void displayQuestion(String question) {
        System.out.println(question);
    }
    private static String getUserAnswer() {
        System.out.print("Your answer: ");
        return scanner.nextLine();
    }
    private static boolean checkAnswer(String question, String userAnswer) {
        return answers.containsKey(question) &&
answers.get(question).equalsIgnoreCase(userAnswer);
    }
    private static void displayFinalScore() {
        System.out.println("Quiz complete! Here is your final score:");
        System.out.println("Score: " + score + " out of " + questions.size());
    }
}
```

21. Falling Blocks Game

```
import java.util.*;
public class FallingBlocksGame {
    private static final int ROWS = 10;
    private static final int COLS = 10;
    private static final char EMPTY_CHAR = '.';
    private static final char BLOCK_CHAR = '#';
    private static final char PLAYER_CHAR = '^';
    private static char[][] grid;
    private static int playerPos;
    private static int score;
    private static Random random = new Random();
    private static Scanner scanner = new Scanner(System.in);
    public static void main(String[] args) {
        System.out.println("Welcome to Falling Blocks Game!");
        System.out.println("Catch as many blocks (\"#\") as you can with your paddle (\"^\").\n");
        initializeGame();
        while (true) {
            displayGrid();
            handlePlayerInput();
            updateGame();
            if (isGameOver()) {
                System.out.println("\nGame Over! Final Score: " + score);
                break;
            }
        }
        scanner.close();
    }
    private static void initializeGame() {
        grid = new char[ROWS][COLS];
        playerPos = COLS / 2;
        score = 0;
        for (int row = 0; row < ROWS; row++) {
```

```
            Arrays.fill(grid[row], EMPTY_CHAR);
        }
    }
    private static void displayGrid() {
        for (int row = 0; row < ROWS; row++) {
            for (int col = 0; col < COLS; col++) {
                System.out.print(grid[row][col] + " ");
            }
            System.out.println();
        }
        System.out.println();
    }
    private static void handlePlayerInput() {
        System.out.print("Move paddle left (L) or right (R): ");
        String input = scanner.nextLine().toUpperCase();
        if (input.equals("L") && playerPos > 0) {
            playerPos--;
        } else if (input.equals("R") && playerPos < COLS - 1) {
            playerPos++;
        }
    }
    private static void updateGame() {
        // Shift grid down
        for (int row = ROWS - 1; row > 0; row--) {
            for (int col = 0; col < COLS; col++) {
                grid[row][col] = grid[row - 1][col];
            }
        }
        // Generate new row at the top
        for (int col = 0; col < COLS; col++) {
            grid[0][col] = (random.nextInt(2) == 0) ? EMPTY_CHAR : BLOCK_CHAR;
        }
        // Check if player catches a block
```

```
        if (grid[ROWS - 1][playerPos] == BLOCK_CHAR) {
            score++;
        }
    }
    private static boolean isGameOver() {
        return grid[ROWS - 1][playerPos] == BLOCK_CHAR;
    }
}
```

22. Simple Racing Game

```
import java.util.*;
public class SimpleRacingGame {
    private static final int TRACK_LENGTH = 20;
    private static final int PLAYER_START = 1;
    private static final int OPPONENTS = 3;
    private static final char PLAYER_CHAR = 'P';
    private static final char OPPONENT_CHAR = 'C';
    private static final char TRACK_CHAR = '-';
    private static char[] track;
    private static int playerPosition;
    private static int[] opponentPositions;
    private static Random random = new Random();
    private static Scanner scanner = new Scanner(System.in);
    public static void main(String[] args) {
        System.out.println("Welcome to Simple Racing Game!");
        System.out.println("Get ready to race!\n");
        initializeGame();
        while (true) {
            displayTrack();
            handlePlayerMove();
            moveOpponents();
            if (checkWin()) {
                System.out.println("\nCongratulations! You won the race!");
                break;
            }
        }
        scanner.close();
    }
    private static void initializeGame() {
        track = new char[TRACK_LENGTH];
        Arrays.fill(track, TRACK_CHAR);
        track[0] = PLAYER_CHAR;
```

```
        playerPosition = PLAYER_START;
        opponentPositions = new int[OPPONENTS];
        for (int i = 0; i < OPPONENTS; i++) {
            opponentPositions[i] = PLAYER_START;
            track[PLAYER_START] = OPPONENT_CHAR;
        }
    }
    private static void displayTrack() {
        for (char cell : track) {
            System.out.print(cell);
        }
        System.out.println(); // Move to next line after printing track
    }
    private static void handlePlayerMove() {
        System.out.print("Press Enter to move forward...");
        scanner.nextLine(); // Wait for player to press Enter
        track[playerPosition] = TRACK_CHAR; // Clear current position
        playerPosition++; // Move player forward
        track[playerPosition] = PLAYER_CHAR; // Update new position
    }
    private static void moveOpponents() {
        for (int i = 0; i < OPPONENTS; i++) {
            if (random.nextBoolean()) { // Randomly decide to move opponent forward
                track[opponentPositions[i]] = TRACK_CHAR; // Clear current position
                opponentPositions[i]++; // Move opponent forward
                track[opponentPositions[i]] = OPPONENT_CHAR; // Update new position
            }
        }
    }
    private static boolean checkWin() {
        if (playerPosition >= TRACK_LENGTH - 1) {
            return true; // Player reached the finish line
        }
```

```
        for (int opponentPosition : opponentPositions) {
            if (opponentPosition >= TRACK_LENGTH - 1) {
                return true; // One of the opponents reached the finish line
            }
        }
        return false;
    }
}
```

23. Word Search Puzzle

```
import java.util.*;
public class WordSearchPuzzle {
    private static final int GRID_SIZE = 8; // Size of the word search grid (8x8 grid)
    private static final char[][] grid = new char[GRID_SIZE][GRID_SIZE];
    private static final Scanner scanner = new Scanner(System.in);
    private static final List<String> words = Arrays.asList(
        "JAVA", "PYTHON", "CPLUSPLUS", "JAVASCRIPT", "RUBY", "SCALA", "KOTLIN"
    );
    public static void main(String[] args) {
        System.out.println("Welcome to Word Search Puzzle!");
        System.out.println("Find the following words in the grid:");
        for (String word : words) {
            System.out.println("- " + word);
        }
        initializeGrid();
        displayGrid();
        while (!words.isEmpty()) {
            System.out.print("Enter a word to search (or type 'exit' to quit): ");
            String userInput = scanner.nextLine().toUpperCase();
            if (userInput.equals("EXIT")) {
                System.out.println("Thanks for playing!");
                break;
            }
            if (words.contains(userInput)) {
                if (findWord(userInput)) {
                    System.out.println("Congratulations! Found the word: " + userInput);
                    words.remove(userInput);
                } else {
                    System.out.println("Word not found in the grid. Try again.");
                }
            } else {
                System.out.println("Invalid word. Please try again.");
```

```
            }
        }
        scanner.close();
    }
    private static void initializeGrid() {
        Random random = new Random();
        String alphabet = "ABCDEFGHIJKLMNOPQRSTUVWXYZ";
        for (int i = 0; i < GRID_SIZE; i++) {
            for (int j = 0; j < GRID_SIZE; j++) {
                grid[i][j] = alphabet.charAt(random.nextInt(alphabet.length()));
            }
        }
        // Place words in the grid
        for (String word : words) {
            placeWord(word);
        }
    }
    private static void placeWord(String word) {
        Random random = new Random();
        int direction = random.nextInt(8); // 8 possible directions
        int startX, startY;
        do {
            startX = random.nextInt(GRID_SIZE);
            startY = random.nextInt(GRID_SIZE);
        } while (!canPlaceWord(word, startX, startY, direction));
        // Place word in the grid
        int deltaX = 0, deltaY = 0;
        switch (direction) {
            case 0: deltaY = 1; break; // Horizontal (left to right)
            case 1: deltaX = 1; break; // Vertical (top to bottom)
            case 2: deltaX = 1; deltaY = 1; break; // Diagonal (top-left to bottom-right)
            case 3: deltaX = 1; deltaY = -1; break; // Diagonal (bottom-left to top-right)
            case 4: deltaY = -1; break; // Horizontal (right to left)
```

```
            case 5: deltaX = -1; break; // Vertical (bottom to top)
            case 6: deltaX = -1; deltaY = -1; break; // Diagonal (bottom-right to top-left)
            case 7: deltaX = -1; deltaY = 1; break; // Diagonal (top-right to bottom-left)
        }
        int x = startX, y = startY;
        for (char letter : word.toCharArray()) {
            grid[x][y] = letter;
            x += deltaX;
            y += deltaY;
        }
    }
    private static boolean canPlaceWord(String word, int startX, int startY, int direction) {
        int length = word.length();
        int deltaX = 0, deltaY = 0;
        switch (direction) {
            case 0: deltaY = 1; break; // Horizontal (left to right)
            case 1: deltaX = 1; break; // Vertical (top to bottom)
            case 2: deltaX = 1; deltaY = 1; break; // Diagonal (top-left to bottom-right)
            case 3: deltaX = 1; deltaY = -1; break; // Diagonal (bottom-left to top-right)
            case 4: deltaY = -1; break; // Horizontal (right to left)
            case 5: deltaX = -1; break; // Vertical (bottom to top)
            case 6: deltaX = -1; deltaY = -1; break; // Diagonal (bottom-right to top-left)
            case 7: deltaX = -1; deltaY = 1; break; // Diagonal (top-right to bottom-left)
        }
        int x = startX, y = startY;
        for (char letter : word.toCharArray()) {
            if (x < 0 || x >= GRID_SIZE || y < 0 || y >= GRID_SIZE || (grid[x][y] != 0 && grid[x][y]
!= letter)) {
                return false;
            }
            x += deltaX;
            y += deltaY;
        }
```

```
        return true;
    }
    private static boolean findWord(String word) {
        int[][] directions = {
            {0, 1}, {1, 0}, {1, 1}, {1, -1},
            {0, -1}, {-1, 0}, {-1, -1}, {-1, 1}
        };
        for (int i = 0; i < GRID_SIZE; i++) {
            for (int j = 0; j < GRID_SIZE; j++) {
                if (grid[i][j] == word.charAt(0)) {
                    for (int[] dir : directions) {
                        if (checkDirection(word, i, j, dir[0], dir[1])) {
                            return true;
                        }
                    }
                }
            }
        }
        return false;
    }
    private static boolean checkDirection(String word, int startX, int startY, int deltaX, int
deltaY) {
        int x = startX, y = startY;
        for (char letter : word.toCharArray()) {
            if (x < 0 || x >= GRID_SIZE || y < 0 || y >= GRID_SIZE || grid[x][y] != letter) {
                return false;
            }
            x += deltaX;
            y += deltaY;
        }
        return true;
    }
```

```
    private static void displayGrid() {
        System.out.println("Word Search Puzzle:");
        for (char[] row : grid) {
            System.out.println(Arrays.toString(row));
        }
        System.out.println();
    }
}
```

24. Simple Chess Game

```
import java.util.*;
public class SimpleChessGame {
    private static final int BOARD_SIZE = 8;
    private static char[][] board = new char[BOARD_SIZE][BOARD_SIZE];
    private static Scanner scanner = new Scanner(System.in);
    private static boolean isWhiteTurn = true;
    public static void main(String[] args) {
        initializeBoard();
        boolean isGameOver = false;
        while (!isGameOver) {
            displayBoard();
            char playerColor = isWhiteTurn ? 'W' : 'B';
            System.out.println("Player " + playerColor + "'s turn.");
            if (isCheckMate(!isWhiteTurn)) {
                System.out.println("Checkmate! Player " + playerColor + " wins.");
                isGameOver = true;
                continue;
            }
            if (isStalemate(!isWhiteTurn)) {
                System.out.println("Stalemate! It's a draw.");
                isGameOver = true;
                continue;
            }
            System.out.print("Enter move (e.g., e2-e4): ");
            String move = scanner.nextLine().trim().toLowerCase();
            if (isValidMove(move)) {
                makeMove(move);
                isWhiteTurn = !isWhiteTurn; // Switch turns
            } else {
                System.out.println("Invalid move. Try again.");
            }
        }
```

```
        scanner.close();
    }
    private static void initializeBoard() {
        // Initialize the chessboard with pieces
        for (int row = 0; row < BOARD_SIZE; row++) {
            for (int col = 0; col < BOARD_SIZE; col++) {
                if (row == 0 || row == BOARD_SIZE - 1) {
                    // Place black and white pieces on the first and last rows
                    char piece = (row == 0) ? 'b' : 'w';
                    switch (col) {
                        case 0:
                        case 7:
                            board[row][col] = (piece == 'b') ? 'r' : 'R'; // rook
                            break;
                        case 1:
                        case 6:
                            board[row][col] = (piece == 'b') ? 'n' : 'N'; // knight
                            break;
                        case 2:
                        case 5:
                            board[row][col] = (piece == 'b') ? 'b' : 'B'; // bishop
                            break;
                        case 3:
                            board[row][col] = (piece == 'b') ? 'q' : 'Q'; // queen
                            break;
                        case 4:
                            board[row][col] = (piece == 'b') ? 'k' : 'K'; // king
                            break;
                    }
                } else if (row == 1 || row == BOARD_SIZE - 2) {
                    board[row][col] = (row == 1) ? 'p' : 'P'; // pawn
                } else {
                    board[row][col] = '.'; // empty space
```

```
                }
            }
        }
    }
    private static void displayBoard() {
        // Display the current state of the chessboard
        for (int row = 0; row < BOARD_SIZE; row++) {
            for (int col = 0; col < BOARD_SIZE; col++) {
                System.out.print(board[row][col] + " ");
            }
            System.out.println();
        }
    }
    private static boolean isValidMove(String move) {
        // Validate the player's move input
        if (move.length() != 5) return false;
        int startRow = BOARD_SIZE - (move.charAt(1) - '1') - 1;
        int startCol = move.charAt(0) - 'a';
        int endRow = BOARD_SIZE - (move.charAt(4) - '1') - 1;
        int endCol = move.charAt(3) - 'a';
        if (startRow < 0 || startRow >= BOARD_SIZE || startCol < 0 || startCol >= BOARD_SIZE ||
            endRow < 0 || endRow >= BOARD_SIZE || endCol < 0 || endCol >= BOARD_SIZE) {
            return false;
        }
        char piece = board[startRow][startCol];
        char targetPiece = board[endRow][endCol];
        boolean isWhitePiece = Character.isUpperCase(piece);
        // Check if the move is valid based on the piece type
        switch (Character.toLowerCase(piece)) {
            case 'p': // pawn
                // TODO: Implement pawn movement rules
                break;
            case 'r': // rook
```

```
            // TODO: Implement rook movement rules
            break;
        case 'n': // knight
            // TODO: Implement knight movement rules
            break;
        case 'b': // bishop
            // TODO: Implement bishop movement rules
            break;
        case 'q': // queen
            // TODO: Implement queen movement rules
            break;
        case 'k': // king
            // TODO: Implement king movement rules
            break;
        default:
            return false;
    }
    return true;
}
private static void makeMove(String move) {
    // Update the chessboard after making a valid move
    int startRow = BOARD_SIZE - (move.charAt(1) - '1') - 1;
    int startCol = move.charAt(0) - 'a';
    int endRow = BOARD_SIZE - (move.charAt(4) - '1') - 1;
    int endCol = move.charAt(3) - 'a';
    board[endRow][endCol] = board[startRow][startCol];
    board[startRow][startCol] = '.';
}
private static boolean isCheckMate(boolean isWhite) {
    // Check if the opponent's king is in checkmate
    // TODO: Implement checkmate detection logic
    return false;
}
```

```
    private static boolean isStalemate(boolean isWhite) {
        // Check if the game is in stalemate (no legal moves available)
        // TODO: Implement stalemate detection logic
        return false;
    }
}
```

25. Mastermind Game

```
import java.util.*;
public class MastermindGame {
    private static final int CODE_LENGTH = 4; // Length of the secret code
    private static final int MAX_ATTEMPTS = 10; // Maximum number of attempts allowed
    private static final char[] COLORS = {'R', 'G', 'B', 'Y', 'O', 'P'}; // Available colors
    private static char[] secretCode;
    private static Scanner scanner = new Scanner(System.in);
    public static void main(String[] args) {
        System.out.println("Welcome to Mastermind!");
        // Generate a random secret code
        generateSecretCode();
        // Start the game loop
        boolean isGameOver = false;
        for (int attempt = 1; attempt <= MAX_ATTEMPTS; attempt++) {
            System.out.println("\nAttempt " + attempt + " of " + MAX_ATTEMPTS);
            char[] guess = getGuess();
            if (checkGuess(guess)) {
                System.out.println("Congratulations! You guessed the secret code.");
                isGameOver = true;
                break;
            } else {
                displayFeedback(guess);
            }
        }
        if (!isGameOver) {
            System.out.println("\nOut of attempts. The secret code was: " +
Arrays.toString(secretCode));
        }
        scanner.close();
    }
    private static void generateSecretCode() {
        Random random = new Random();
```

```
        secretCode = new char[CODE_LENGTH];
        for (int i = 0; i < CODE_LENGTH; i++) {
            secretCode[i] = COLORS[random.nextInt(COLORS.length)];
        }
    }
    private static char[] getGuess() {
        System.out.println("Enter your guess (e.g., RGBY): ");
        String input = scanner.nextLine().toUpperCase();
        // Validate the input and convert to char array
        while (input.length() != CODE_LENGTH || !isValidGuess(input)) {
            System.out.println("Invalid input. Please enter a " + CODE_LENGTH + "-character
guess using colors (RGBYOP): ");
            input = scanner.nextLine().toUpperCase();
        }
        return input.toCharArray();
    }
    private static boolean isValidGuess(String guess) {
        for (char c : guess.toCharArray()) {
            if (!Arrays.toString(COLORS).contains(Character.toString(c))) {
                return false;
            }
        }
        return true;
    }
    private static boolean checkGuess(char[] guess) {
        return Arrays.equals(guess, secretCode);
    }
    private static void displayFeedback(char[] guess) {
        int exactMatches = 0;
        int colorMatches = 0;
        boolean[] visited = new boolean[CODE_LENGTH];
        // Count exact matches
        for (int i = 0; i < CODE_LENGTH; i++) {
```

```
        if (guess[i] == secretCode[i]) {
            exactMatches++;
            visited[i] = true;
        }
    }
    // Count color matches (ignoring exact matches)
    for (int i = 0; i < CODE_LENGTH; i++) {
        if (!visited[i]) {
            for (int j = 0; j < CODE_LENGTH; j++) {
                if (i != j && guess[i] == secretCode[j] && !visited[j]) {
                    colorMatches++;
                    visited[j] = true;
                    break;
                }
            }
        }
    }
    System.out.println("Feedback:");
    System.out.println("Exact matches: " + exactMatches);
    System.out.println("Color matches: " + colorMatches);
  }
}
```

26. Text-Based RPG Adventure

```
import java.util.*;
public class TextBasedRPGAdventure {
    private static final Scanner scanner = new Scanner(System.in);
    private static Random random = new Random();
    private static int playerHealth = 100;
    private static int enemyHealth = 50;
    private static int potions = 3;
    public static void main(String[] args) {
        System.out.println("Welcome to the Text-Based RPG Adventure!");
        System.out.println("You find yourself in a dark dungeon...");
        while (playerHealth > 0) {
            System.out.println("\n-------------------");
            System.out.println("Current Stats:");
            System.out.println("Player Health: " + playerHealth);
            System.out.println("Potions: " + potions);
            System.out.println("-------------------");
            System.out.println("\nWhat would you like to do?");
            System.out.println("1. Explore the room");
            System.out.println("2. Drink a potion");
            System.out.println("3. Quit the game");
            int choice = getUserChoice(1, 3);
            switch (choice) {
                case 1:
                    exploreRoom();
                    break;
                case 2:
                    usePotion();
                    break;
                case 3:
                    endGame();
                    return;
            }
```

```
        if (enemyHealth > 0) {
          System.out.println("\n-------------------");
          System.out.println("A wild monster appears! Defeat it!");
          System.out.println("-------------------");
          battle();
        }
        if (playerHealth <= 0) {
          System.out.println("\nGame Over! You have been defeated.");
          endGame();
          return;
        }
      }
    }
    private static int getUserChoice(int min, int max) {
      int choice;
      do {
        System.out.print("Enter your choice: ");
        while (!scanner.hasNextInt()) {
          System.out.println("Invalid input! Please enter a number.");
          scanner.next();
        }
        choice = scanner.nextInt();
      } while (choice < min || choice > max);
      scanner.nextLine(); // Consume newline
      return choice;
    }
    private static void exploreRoom() {
      int chance = random.nextInt(4); // 25% chance of encountering an enemy
      if (chance == 0) {
        System.out.println("You found a treasure chest!");
        System.out.println("You gain 20 health.");
        playerHealth += 20;
      } else {
```

```
            System.out.println("You search the room but find nothing of interest.");
        }
    }
    private static void usePotion() {
        if (potions > 0) {
            System.out.println("You drink a healing potion.");
            playerHealth += 30;
            potions--;
        } else {
            System.out.println("You have no potions left!");
        }
    }
    private static void battle() {
        while (playerHealth > 0 && enemyHealth > 0) {
            System.out.println("\n1. Attack");
            System.out.println("2. Defend");
            int choice = getUserChoice(1, 2);
            if (choice == 1) {
                // Player attacks
                int damage = random.nextInt(10) + 10; // Random damage between 10 to 19
                System.out.println("You attack the monster for " + damage + " damage.");
                enemyHealth -= damage;
            } else {
                // Monster attacks
                int damage = random.nextInt(8) + 5; // Random damage between 5 to 12
                System.out.println("The monster attacks you for " + damage + " damage.");
                playerHealth -= damage;
            }
            // Display current health
            System.out.println("Player Health: " + playerHealth);
            System.out.println("Monster Health: " + enemyHealth);
        }
        if (playerHealth > 0) {
```

```
            System.out.println("You defeated the monster!");
            enemyHealth = 50; // Reset enemy health
        } else {
            System.out.println("You were defeated by the monster.");
        }
    }
    private static void endGame() {
        System.out.println("Thank you for playing!");
        scanner.close();
        System.exit(0);
    }
}
```

27. Simple Simon Game

```
import java.util.*;
public class SimpleSimonGame {
    private static final String[] COLORS = {"RED", "GREEN", "BLUE", "YELLOW"};
    private static final int SEQUENCE_LENGTH = 10; // Length of the sequence to remember
    private static final int DELAY_MS = 1000; // Delay between each step in milliseconds
    private static List<String> sequence = new ArrayList<>();
    private static Scanner scanner = new Scanner(System.in);
    public static void main(String[] args) {
        System.out.println("Welcome to Simple Simon!");
        // Play the game
        boolean isGameOver = false;
        while (!isGameOver) {
            generateSequence();
            displaySequence();
            // Get player input
            for (int i = 0; i < sequence.size(); i++) {
                System.out.print("Enter color " + (i + 1) + ": ");
                String playerInput = scanner.nextLine().trim().toUpperCase();
                if (!playerInput.equals(sequence.get(i))) {
                    System.out.println("Incorrect! Game Over.");
                    isGameOver = true;
                    break;
                }
                // Delay before showing the next color
                try {
                    Thread.sleep(DELAY_MS);
                } catch (InterruptedException e) {
                    e.printStackTrace();
                }
            }
            if (!isGameOver) {
                System.out.println("Congratulations! You completed the sequence.");
```

```
            }
            System.out.print("Play again? (yes/no): ");
            String playAgain = scanner.nextLine().trim().toLowerCase();
            if (!playAgain.equals("yes")) {
                isGameOver = true;
            }
        }
        scanner.close();
        System.out.println("Thanks for playing Simple Simon!");
    }
    private static void generateSequence() {
        Random random = new Random();
        sequence.clear();
        for (int i = 0; i < SEQUENCE_LENGTH; i++) {
            sequence.add(COLORS[random.nextInt(COLORS.length)]);
        }
    }
    private static void displaySequence() {
        System.out.println("Memorize the sequence:");
        for (int i = 0; i < sequence.size(); i++) {
            System.out.println((i + 1) + ". " + sequence.get(i));
            try {
                Thread.sleep(DELAY_MS);
            } catch (InterruptedException e) {
                e.printStackTrace();
            }
        }
        System.out.println("Now repeat the sequence.");
    }
}
```

28. Frogger-style Game

```
import java.util.*;
public class FroggerGame {
    private static final int GRID_SIZE = 10;
    private static final char FROG_CHAR = '@';
    private static final char ROAD_CHAR = '_';
    private static final char CAR_CHAR = '#';
    private static char[][] grid = new char[GRID_SIZE][GRID_SIZE];
    private static int frogRow;
    private static int frogCol;
    private static boolean isGameOver = false;
    private static Scanner scanner = new Scanner(System.in);
    public static void main(String[] args) {
        System.out.println("Welcome to Frogger!");
        initializeGrid();
        displayGrid();
        while (!isGameOver) {
            System.out.print("Enter your move (w/a/s/d): ");
            char move = scanner.next().charAt(0);
            handleMove(move);
            displayGrid();
            if (frogRow == 0) {
                System.out.println("Congratulations! You reached the other side safely.");
                isGameOver = true;
            } else if (grid[frogRow][frogCol] == CAR_CHAR) {
                System.out.println("Game over! You got hit by a car.");
                isGameOver = true;
            }
        }
        scanner.close();
    }
    private static void initializeGrid() {
        // Initialize the grid with road and cars
```

```
        Random random = new Random();
        for (int row = 0; row < GRID_SIZE; row++) {
            for (int col = 0; col < GRID_SIZE; col++) {
                if (row == GRID_SIZE - 1) {
                    grid[row][col] = ROAD_CHAR; // Bottom row is road
                } else {
                    grid[row][col] = (random.nextInt(4) == 0) ? CAR_CHAR : ROAD_CHAR;
                }
            }
        }
        // Place the frog at the start position
        frogRow = GRID_SIZE - 1;
        frogCol = GRID_SIZE / 2;
        grid[frogRow][frogCol] = FROG_CHAR;
    }
    private static void displayGrid() {
        // Display the grid
        for (int row = 0; row < GRID_SIZE; row++) {
            for (int col = 0; col < GRID_SIZE; col++) {
                System.out.print(grid[row][col] + " ");
            }
            System.out.println();
        }
    }
    private static void handleMove(char move) {
        // Move the frog based on user input
        switch (move) {
            case 'w':
                if (frogRow > 0) {
                    grid[frogRow][frogCol] = ROAD_CHAR;
                    frogRow--;
                    grid[frogRow][frogCol] = FROG_CHAR;
                }
```

```
            break;
        case 's':
            if (frogRow < GRID_SIZE - 1) {
                grid[frogRow][frogCol] = ROAD_CHAR;
                frogRow++;
                grid[frogRow][frogCol] = FROG_CHAR;
            }
            break;
        case 'a':
            if (frogCol > 0) {
                grid[frogRow][frogCol] = ROAD_CHAR;
                frogCol--;
                grid[frogRow][frogCol] = FROG_CHAR;
            }
            break;
        case 'd':
            if (frogCol < GRID_SIZE - 1) {
                grid[frogRow][frogCol] = ROAD_CHAR;
                frogCol++;
                grid[frogRow][frogCol] = FROG_CHAR;
            }
            break;
        default:
            System.out.println("Invalid move. Use 'w' (up), 's' (down), 'a' (left), 'd' (right).");
            break;
    }
  }
}
```

29. Hangman with Graphics

```
import java.util.*;
public class HangmanGame {
   private static final String[] WORDS = {"JAVA", "PYTHON", "PROGRAMMING",
"COMPUTER", "ALGORITHM", "DEVELOPER"};
   private static final String[] HANGMAN_ASCII = {
      "  +---+\n" +
      "  |   |\n" +
      "      |\n" +
      "      |\n" +
      "      |\n" +
      "      |\n" +
      "=========",
      "  +---+\n" +
      "  |   |\n" +
      "  O   |\n" +
      "      |\n" +
      "      |\n" +
      "      |\n" +
      "=========",
      "  +---+\n" +
      "  |   |\n" +
      "  O   |\n" +
      "  |   |\n" +
      "      |\n" +
      "      |\n" +
      "=========",
      "  +---+\n" +
      "  |   |\n" +
      "  O   |\n" +
      " /|   |\n" +
      "      |\n" +
      "      |\n" +
```

```
        "=========",
        "  +---+\n" +
        "  |   |\n" +
        "  O   |\n" +
        " /|\\  |\n" +
        "      |\n" +
        "      |\n" +
        "=========",
        "  +---+\n" +
        "  |   |\n" +
        "  O   |\n" +
        " /|\\  |\n" +
        " /    |\n" +
        "      |\n" +
        "=========",
        "  +---+\n" +
        "  |   |\n" +
        "  O   |\n" +
        " /|\\  |\n" +
        " / \\  |\n" +
        "      |\n" +
        "========="
    };
    private static Random random = new Random();
    private static String secretWord;
    private static char[] guessedLetters;
    private static Set<Character> incorrectGuesses = new HashSet<>();
    private static int incorrectAttempts = 0;
    private static Scanner scanner = new Scanner(System.in);
    public static void main(String[] args) {
        System.out.println("Welcome to Hangman!");
        // Select a random word from the WORDS array
        secretWord = WORDS[random.nextInt(WORDS.length)];
```

```
        guessedLetters = new char[secretWord.length()];
        // Initialize guessedLetters array with underscores
        Arrays.fill(guessedLetters, '_');
        // Start the game loop
        while (true) {
            displayHangman();
            displayWord();
            if (Arrays.equals(guessedLetters, secretWord.toCharArray())) {
                System.out.println("Congratulations! You guessed the word: " + secretWord);
                break;
            }
            System.out.print("\nEnter a letter: ");
            char guess = scanner.next().toUpperCase().charAt(0);
            if (secretWord.contains(String.valueOf(guess))) {
                updateGuessedLetters(guess);
            } else {
                incorrectGuesses.add(guess);
                incorrectAttempts++;
            }
            if (incorrectAttempts == HANGMAN_ASCII.length - 1) {
                displayHangman();
                System.out.println("You lost! The word was: " + secretWord);
                break;
            }
        }
        scanner.close();
    }
    private static void displayHangman() {
        System.out.println("\nIncorrect attempts: " + incorrectAttempts);
        System.out.println(HANGMAN_ASCII[incorrectAttempts]);
    }
    private static void displayWord() {
        System.out.print("Current word: ");
```

```
        for (char c : guessedLetters) {
            System.out.print(c + " ");
        }
        System.out.println();
        System.out.print("Incorrect guesses: ");
        for (char c : incorrectGuesses) {
            System.out.print(c + " ");
        }
        System.out.println();
    }
    private static void updateGuessedLetters(char guess) {
        for (int i = 0; i < secretWord.length(); i++) {
            if (secretWord.charAt(i) == guess) {
                guessedLetters[i] = guess;
            }
        }
    }
}
```

30. Puzzle Slider Game

```
import java.util.*;
public class PuzzleSliderGame {
    private static final int GRID_SIZE = 3; // Size of the puzzle grid (e.g., 3x3)
    private static final int EMPTY_TILE = 0; // Value representing the empty tile
    private static final int MAX_MOVES = 50; // Maximum number of moves allowed
    private static final int[][] WINNING_GRID = {
        {1, 2, 3},
        {4, 5, 6},
        {7, 8, EMPTY_TILE}
    };
    private static int[][] grid = new int[GRID_SIZE][GRID_SIZE];
    private static int emptyRow;
    private static int emptyCol;
    private static Scanner scanner = new Scanner(System.in);
    private static Random random = new Random();
    public static void main(String[] args) {
        System.out.println("Welcome to Puzzle Slider!");
        initializeGrid();
        displayGrid();
        int moves = 0;
        while (moves < MAX_MOVES) {
            System.out.println("\nEnter your move (w/a/s/d) or 'q' to quit: ");
            String move = scanner.next().toLowerCase();
            if (move.equals("q")) {
                System.out.println("Game ended. Thanks for playing!");
                break;
            }
            if (isValidMove(move)) {
                makeMove(move);
                moves++;
                displayGrid();
                if (isGameOver()) {
```

```
                System.out.println("Congratulations! You solved the puzzle!");
                break;
            }
        } else {
            System.out.println("Invalid move. Use 'w' (up), 'a' (left), 's' (down), 'd' (right).");
        }
    }
    if (moves >= MAX_MOVES) {
        System.out.println("Out of moves! Game over.");
    }
    scanner.close();
}
private static void initializeGrid() {
    List<Integer> numbers = new ArrayList<>();
    for (int i = 1; i < GRID_SIZE * GRID_SIZE; i++) {
        numbers.add(i);
    }
    numbers.add(EMPTY_TILE);
    Collections.shuffle(numbers);
    int index = 0;
    for (int row = 0; row < GRID_SIZE; row++) {
        for (int col = 0; col < GRID_SIZE; col++) {
            grid[row][col] = numbers.get(index++);
            if (grid[row][col] == EMPTY_TILE) {
                emptyRow = row;
                emptyCol = col;
            }
        }
    }
}
private static void displayGrid() {
    System.out.println("Current Grid:");
    for (int[] row : grid) {
```

```
        for (int num : row) {
          if (num == EMPTY_TILE) {
            System.out.print("  ");
          } else {
            System.out.print(num + " ");
          }
        }
        System.out.println();
      }
    }
    private static boolean isValidMove(String move) {
      switch (move) {
        case "w":
          return emptyRow > 0;
        case "a":
          return emptyCol > 0;
        case "s":
          return emptyRow < GRID_SIZE - 1;
        case "d":
          return emptyCol < GRID_SIZE - 1;
        default:
          return false;
      }
    }
    private static void makeMove(String move) {
      switch (move) {
        case "w": // Move empty tile up
          swapTiles(emptyRow, emptyCol, emptyRow - 1, emptyCol);
          emptyRow--;
          break;
        case "a": // Move empty tile left
          swapTiles(emptyRow, emptyCol, emptyRow, emptyCol - 1);
          emptyCol--;
```

```
            break;
        case "s": // Move empty tile down
            swapTiles(emptyRow, emptyCol, emptyRow + 1, emptyCol);
            emptyRow++;
            break;
        case "d": // Move empty tile right
            swapTiles(emptyRow, emptyCol, emptyRow, emptyCol + 1);
            emptyCol++;
            break;
        }
    }
    private static void swapTiles(int row1, int col1, int row2, int col2) {
        int temp = grid[row1][col1];
        grid[row1][col1] = grid[row2][col2];
        grid[row2][col2] = temp;
    }
    private static boolean isGameOver() {
        for (int row = 0; row < GRID_SIZE; row++) {
            for (int col = 0; col < GRID_SIZE; col++) {
                if (grid[row][col] != WINNING_GRID[row][col]) {
                    return false;
                }
            }
        }
        return true;
    }
}
```

31. Jigsaw Puzzle Game

```
import java.util.*;
public class JigsawPuzzleGame {
    private static final int PUZZLE_SIZE = 3; // Size of the puzzle (e.g., 3x3)
    private static final int MAX_MOVES = 50; // Maximum number of moves allowed
    private static int[][] puzzleBoard = new int[PUZZLE_SIZE][PUZZLE_SIZE];
    private static int[][] solutionBoard = {
        {1, 2, 3},
        {4, 5, 6},
        {7, 8, 0}
    };
    private static int emptyRow;
    private static int emptyCol;
    private static Scanner scanner = new Scanner(System.in);
    public static void main(String[] args) {
        System.out.println("Welcome to Jigsaw Puzzle!");
        initializePuzzle();
        displayPuzzle();
        int moves = 0;
        while (moves < MAX_MOVES) {
            System.out.println("\nEnter your move (w/a/s/d) or 'q' to quit: ");
            String move = scanner.next().toLowerCase();
            if (move.equals("q")) {
                System.out.println("Game ended. Thanks for playing!");
                break;
            }
            if (isValidMove(move)) {
                makeMove(move);
                moves++;
                displayPuzzle();
                if (isPuzzleSolved()) {
                    System.out.println("Congratulations! You solved the puzzle!");
                    break;
```

```
            }
        } else {
            System.out.println("Invalid move. Use 'w' (up), 'a' (left), 's' (down), 'd' (right).");
        }
    }
    if (moves >= MAX_MOVES) {
        System.out.println("Out of moves! Game over.");
    }
    scanner.close();
}
private static void initializePuzzle() {
    List<Integer> numbers = new ArrayList<>();
    for (int i = 1; i < PUZZLE_SIZE * PUZZLE_SIZE; i++) {
        numbers.add(i);
    }
    numbers.add(0); // 0 represents the empty space
    Collections.shuffle(numbers);
    int index = 0;
    for (int row = 0; row < PUZZLE_SIZE; row++) {
        for (int col = 0; col < PUZZLE_SIZE; col++) {
            puzzleBoard[row][col] = numbers.get(index++);
            if (puzzleBoard[row][col] == 0) {
                emptyRow = row;
                emptyCol = col;
            }
        }
    }
}
private static void displayPuzzle() {
    System.out.println("Current Puzzle:");
    for (int[] row : puzzleBoard) {
        for (int num : row) {
            if (num == 0) {
```

```
                System.out.print("  ");
            } else {
                System.out.print(num + " ");
            }
        }
        System.out.println();
    }
}
private static boolean isValidMove(String move) {
    switch (move) {
        case "w":
            return emptyRow > 0;
        case "a":
            return emptyCol > 0;
        case "s":
            return emptyRow < PUZZLE_SIZE - 1;
        case "d":
            return emptyCol < PUZZLE_SIZE - 1;
        default:
            return false;
    }
}
private static void makeMove(String move) {
    int newRow = emptyRow;
    int newCol = emptyCol;
    switch (move) {
        case "w": // Move empty space up
            newRow = emptyRow - 1;
            break;
        case "a": // Move empty space left
            newCol = emptyCol - 1;
            break;
        case "s": // Move empty space down
```

```
            newRow = emptyRow + 1;
            break;
        case "d": // Move empty space right
            newCol = emptyCol + 1;
            break;
    }
    // Swap empty space with the selected tile
    puzzleBoard[emptyRow][emptyCol] = puzzleBoard[newRow][newCol];
    puzzleBoard[newRow][newCol] = 0;
    // Update empty space position
    emptyRow = newRow;
    emptyCol = newCol;
  }
  private static boolean isPuzzleSolved() {
    for (int row = 0; row < PUZZLE_SIZE; row++) {
      for (int col = 0; col < PUZZLE_SIZE; col++) {
        if (puzzleBoard[row][col] != solutionBoard[row][col]) {
          return false;
        }
      }
    }
    return true;
  }
}
```

32. Sudoku Solver

```
public class SudokuSolver {
    private static final int SIZE = 9;
    private static final int EMPTY = 0;
    public static void main(String[] args) {
        int[][] board = {
            {5, 3, 0, 0, 7, 0, 0, 0, 0},
            {6, 0, 0, 1, 9, 5, 0, 0, 0},
            {0, 9, 8, 0, 0, 0, 0, 6, 0},
            {8, 0, 0, 0, 6, 0, 0, 0, 3},
            {4, 0, 0, 8, 0, 3, 0, 0, 1},
            {7, 0, 0, 0, 2, 0, 0, 0, 6},
            {0, 6, 0, 0, 0, 0, 2, 8, 0},
            {0, 0, 0, 4, 1, 9, 0, 0, 5},
            {0, 0, 0, 0, 8, 0, 0, 7, 9}
        };
        System.out.println("Sudoku board:");
        printBoard(board);
        if (solveSudoku(board)) {
            System.out.println("\nSolved Sudoku board:");
            printBoard(board);
        } else {
            System.out.println("\nNo solution exists for the given Sudoku board.");
        }
    }
    private static boolean solveSudoku(int[][] board) {
        int row = -1;
        int col = -1;
        boolean isEmpty = true;
        // Find the first empty cell
        for (int i = 0; i < SIZE; i++) {
            for (int j = 0; j < SIZE; j++) {
                if (board[i][j] == EMPTY) {
```

```
                row = i;
                col = j;
                isEmpty = false;
                break;
            }
        }
        if (!isEmpty) {
            break;
        }
    }
    // If no empty cell is found, the puzzle is solved
    if (isEmpty) {
        return true;
    }
    // Try placing numbers 1-9 in the empty cell
    for (int num = 1; num <= SIZE; num++) {
        if (isSafe(board, row, col, num)) {
            board[row][col] = num;
            if (solveSudoku(board)) {
                return true;
            } else {
                board[row][col] = EMPTY; // Backtrack
            }
        }
    }
    return false;
}
private static boolean isSafe(int[][] board, int row, int col, int num) {
    // Check if 'num' is not present in the current row
    for (int i = 0; i < SIZE; i++) {
        if (board[row][i] == num) {
            return false;
        }
```

```
        }
        // Check if 'num' is not present in the current column
        for (int i = 0; i < SIZE; i++) {
            if (board[i][col] == num) {
                return false;
            }
        }
        // Check if 'num' is not present in the current 3x3 subgrid
        int startRow = row - row % 3;
        int startCol = col - col % 3;
        for (int i = startRow; i < startRow + 3; i++) {
            for (int j = startCol; j < startCol + 3; j++) {
                if (board[i][j] == num) {
                    return false;
                }
            }
        }
        return true;
    }
    private static void printBoard(int[][] board) {
        for (int i = 0; i < SIZE; i++) {
            for (int j = 0; j < SIZE; j++) {
                System.out.print(board[i][j] + " ");
            }
            System.out.println();
        }
    }
}
```

33. Shooting Gallery Game

```
import java.util.*;
public class ShootingGalleryGame {
   private static final int GAME_DURATION_SECONDS = 30;
   private static final int MAX_TARGETS = 10;
   private static final char TARGET_SYMBOL = '*';
   private static final char EMPTY_SYMBOL = '.';
   private static final Random random = new Random();
   private static final Scanner scanner = new Scanner(System.in);
   public static void main(String[] args) {
      System.out.println("Welcome to the Shooting Gallery Game!");
      System.out.println("Shoot targets ('*') as they appear on the screen.");
      System.out.println("You have " + GAME_DURATION_SECONDS + " seconds to hit as
many targets as you can.");
      char[][] gallery = new char[5][10];
      int targetsHit = 0;
      int totalTargets = 0;
      long startTime = System.currentTimeMillis();
      while (System.currentTimeMillis() - startTime < GAME_DURATION_SECONDS *
1000) {
         if (totalTargets < MAX_TARGETS) {
            generateTarget(gallery);
            totalTargets++;
         }
         displayGallery(gallery);
         System.out.print("Enter target position (row col) or 'q' to quit: ");
         String input = scanner.nextLine().toLowerCase();

         if (input.equals("q")) {
            break;
         }
         String[] parts = input.split(" ");
         if (parts.length == 2) {
```

```
            try {
                int row = Integer.parseInt(parts[0]);
                int col = Integer.parseInt(parts[1]);
                if (row >= 0 && row < gallery.length && col >= 0 && col < gallery[0].length) {
                    if (gallery[row][col] == TARGET_SYMBOL) {
                        System.out.println("Target hit!");
                        targetsHit++;
                    } else {
                        System.out.println("Missed!");
                    }
                    gallery[row][col] = EMPTY_SYMBOL;
                } else {
                    System.out.println("Invalid position. Try again.");
                }
            } catch (NumberFormatException e) {
                System.out.println("Invalid input. Enter row and column numbers.");
            }
        }
    }
    double accuracy = (double) targetsHit / totalTargets * 100;
    System.out.println("\nGame over!");
    System.out.println("Targets hit: " + targetsHit);
    System.out.println("Total targets: " + totalTargets);
    System.out.println("Accuracy: " + String.format("%.2f", accuracy) + "%");
    scanner.close();
}
private static void generateTarget(char[][] gallery) {
    int row = random.nextInt(gallery.length);
    int col = random.nextInt(gallery[0].length);

    if (gallery[row][col] == EMPTY_SYMBOL) {
        gallery[row][col] = TARGET_SYMBOL;
    }
```

```
    }
    private static void displayGallery(char[][] gallery) {
        System.out.println("\nShooting Gallery:");
        for (char[] row : gallery) {
            for (char cell : row) {
                System.out.print(cell + " ");
            }
            System.out.println();
        }
    }
}
```

34. Simon Says Game

```
import java.util.*;
public class SimonSaysGame {
    private static final int MAX_MOVES = 10;
    private static final String[] ACTIONS = {"red", "green", "blue", "yellow"};
    private static final Random random = new Random();
    private static final Scanner scanner = new Scanner(System.in);
    public static void main(String[] args) {
        System.out.println("Welcome to Simon Says!");
        System.out.println("Repeat the sequence of actions.");
        List<String> actionSequence = new ArrayList<>();
        int currentMove = 0;
        boolean gameWon = true;
        // Generate random sequence of actions
        for (int i = 0; i < MAX_MOVES; i++) {
            actionSequence.add(ACTIONS[random.nextInt(ACTIONS.length)]);
        }
        // Show sequence to the player
        System.out.println("Simon says:");
        for (String action : actionSequence) {
            System.out.print(action + " ");
            try {
                Thread.sleep(1000); // Pause between actions
            } catch (InterruptedException e) {
                e.printStackTrace();
            }
        }
        System.out.println("\n");
        // Player repeats the sequence
        for (String expectedAction : actionSequence) {
            System.out.print("Your turn: ");
            String playerAction = scanner.nextLine().trim().toLowerCase();
```

```
        if (!playerAction.equals(expectedAction)) {
            gameWon = false;
            break;
        }
        currentMove++;
    }
    // Display result
    if (gameWon && currentMove == MAX_MOVES) {
        System.out.println("Congratulations! You repeated the sequence correctly!");
    } else {
        System.out.println("Game over! You made a mistake.");
        System.out.println("Correct sequence was:");
        for (String action : actionSequence) {
            System.out.print(action + " ");
        }
        System.out.println();
    }
    scanner.close();
  }
}
```

35. Letter Guessing Game

```
import java.util.*;
public class LetterGuessingGame {
    private static final String[] WORDS = {"apple", "banana", "orange", "mango", "strawberry",
"pineapple"};
    private static final Random random = new Random();
    private static final Scanner scanner = new Scanner(System.in);
    public static void main(String[] args) {
        System.out.println("Welcome to the Letter Guessing Game!");
        System.out.println("Try to guess the secret word by suggesting letters.");
        String secretWord = WORDS[random.nextInt(WORDS.length)];
        StringBuilder guessedWord = new StringBuilder("_".repeat(secretWord.length()));
        Set<Character> guessedLetters = new HashSet<>();
        int attemptsLeft = 7;
        while (attemptsLeft > 0 && !guessedWord.toString().equals(secretWord)) {
            System.out.println("Current word: " + guessedWord);
            System.out.println("Attempts left: " + attemptsLeft);
            System.out.print("Enter a letter: ");
            char guess = scanner.next().toLowerCase().charAt(0);
            if (guessedLetters.contains(guess)) {
                System.out.println("You already guessed '" + guess + "'. Try a different letter.");
                continue;
            }
            guessedLetters.add(guess);
            if (secretWord.contains(String.valueOf(guess))) {
                for (int i = 0; i < secretWord.length(); i++) {
                    if (secretWord.charAt(i) == guess) {
                        guessedWord.setCharAt(i, guess);
                    }
                }
                System.out.println("Good guess!");
            } else {
                System.out.println("Oops! '" + guess + "' is not in the word.");
```

```
                attemptsLeft--;
            }
        }
        if (guessedWord.toString().equals(secretWord)) {
            System.out.println("Congratulations! You guessed the word: " + secretWord);
        } else {
            System.out.println("Out of attempts! The secret word was: " + secretWord);
        }
        scanner.close();
    }
}
```

36. Basketball Shooting Game

```
import java.util.*;
public class BasketballShootingGame {
    private static final int BASKET_HEIGHT = 10; // Height of the basketball hoop
    private static final int MAX_SHOTS = 5; // Maximum number of shots allowed
    private static final int MAX_ANGLE = 90; // Maximum shooting angle in degrees
    private static final int MAX_POWER = 100; // Maximum shooting power
    private static final Random random = new Random();
    private static final Scanner scanner = new Scanner(System.in);
    public static void main(String[] args) {
        System.out.println("Welcome to the Basketball Shooting Game!");
        System.out.println("Try to make successful shots by adjusting the angle and power.");
        int shotsMade = 0;
        while (shotsMade < MAX_SHOTS) {
            int targetAngle = random.nextInt(MAX_ANGLE) + 1;
            int targetDistance = random.nextInt(BASKET_HEIGHT) + 1;
            System.out.println("\nShoot #" + (shotsMade + 1));
            System.out.println("Basket height: " + BASKET_HEIGHT);
            System.out.println("Target distance: " + targetDistance);
            System.out.print("Enter the shooting angle (1-" + MAX_ANGLE + " degrees): ");
            int shootingAngle = scanner.nextInt();
            System.out.print("Enter the shooting power (1-" + MAX_POWER + "): ");
            int shootingPower = scanner.nextInt();
            int actualDistance = calculateShotDistance(shootingAngle, shootingPower);
            if (actualDistance >= targetDistance && shootingAngle == targetAngle) {
                System.out.println("Swish! You made the shot!");
                shotsMade++;
            } else {
                System.out.println("Missed the shot. Try again!");
            }
        }
        System.out.println("\nGame over!");
        System.out.println("Total shots made: " + shotsMade);
```

```
        scanner.close();
    }
    private static int calculateShotDistance(int angle, int power) {
        double radians = Math.toRadians(angle);
        double distance = Math.pow(power, 2) * Math.sin(2 * radians) / 9.8;
        return (int) Math.round(distance);
    }
}
```

37. Simple Physics Simulation

```
import java.util.*;
public class SimplePhysicsSimulation {
  private static final double GRAVITY = 9.8; // Acceleration due to gravity (m/s^2)
  private static final double TIME_STEP = 0.1; // Time step for simulation (seconds)
  public static void main(String[] args) {
    Scanner scanner = new Scanner(System.in);
    System.out.println("Welcome to the Simple Physics Simulation!");
    System.out.println("This program simulates the motion of a projectile under gravity.");
    System.out.print("Enter the initial velocity (m/s): ");
    double initialVelocity = scanner.nextDouble();
    System.out.print("Enter the launch angle (degrees): ");
    double launchAngle = Math.toRadians(scanner.nextDouble());
    simulateProjectile(initialVelocity, launchAngle);
    scanner.close();
  }
  private static void simulateProjectile(double initialVelocity, double launchAngle) {
    double x = 0.0; // Initial x-coordinate
    double y = 0.0; // Initial y-coordinate
    double vx = initialVelocity * Math.cos(launchAngle); // Initial velocity in x-direction
    double vy = initialVelocity * Math.sin(launchAngle); // Initial velocity in y-direction
    System.out.println("\nSimulation Results:");
    while (y >= 0.0) {
      System.out.printf("Time: %.2f s | Position: (%.2f, %.2f) m%n", getTime(x, vx), x, y);
      // Update position and velocity for next time step
      x += vx * TIME_STEP;
      y += vy * TIME_STEP;
      vy -= GRAVITY * TIME_STEP; // Update vertical velocity due to gravity
    }
  }
  private static double getTime(double x, double vx) {
    return x / vx;
  }}
```

38. Leap Year Checker Game

```
import java.util.Scanner;
public class LeapYearChecker {
    public static void main(String[] args) {
        Scanner scanner = new Scanner(System.in);
        System.out.println("Welcome to the Leap Year Checker!");
        System.out.print("Enter a year to check if it's a leap year: ");
        int year = scanner.nextInt();
        if (isLeapYear(year)) {
            System.out.println(year + " is a leap year.");
        } else {
            System.out.println(year + " is not a leap year.");
        }
        scanner.close();
    }
    private static boolean isLeapYear(int year) {
        // Leap year conditions:
        // 1. Year is divisible by 4
        // 2. Year is not divisible by 100 unless it's also divisible by 400
        if (year % 4 == 0) {
            if (year % 100 == 0) {
                if (year % 400 == 0) {
                    return true; // Divisible by 400 -> Leap year
                } else {
                    return false; // Divisible by 100 but not by 400 -> Not a leap year
                }
            } else {
                return true; // Divisible by 4 but not by 100 -> Leap year
            }
        } else {
            return false; // Not divisible by 4 -> Not a leap year
        }
    }}
```

39. Virtual Pet Simulation

```
import java.util.Scanner;
public class VirtualPetSimulation {
    private static final int MAX_HUNGER_LEVEL = 10;
    private static final int MAX_BOREDOM_LEVEL = 10;
    private String petName;
    private int hungerLevel;
    private int boredomLevel;
    public VirtualPetSimulation(String name) {
        this.petName = name;
        this.hungerLevel = 5; // Initial hunger level
        this.boredomLevel = 5; // Initial boredom level
    }
    public void feedPet() {
        if (hungerLevel > 0) {
            hungerLevel--;
            System.out.println(petName + " feels better after eating.");
        } else {
            System.out.println(petName + " is not hungry right now.");
        }
    }
    public void playWithPet() {
        if (boredomLevel > 0) {
            boredomLevel--;
            System.out.println(petName + " enjoys playing with you.");
        } else {
            System.out.println(petName + " is not in the mood to play right now.");
        }
    }
    public void checkStatus() {
        System.out.println("------ " + petName + "'s Status ------");
        System.out.println("Hunger Level: " + hungerLevel);
        System.out.println("Boredom Level: " + boredomLevel);
```

```
        System.out.println("----------------------------");
    }
    public static void main(String[] args) {
        Scanner scanner = new Scanner(System.in);
        System.out.println("Welcome to Virtual Pet Simulation!");
        System.out.print("Enter a name for your pet: ");
        String petName = scanner.nextLine();
        VirtualPetSimulation pet = new VirtualPetSimulation(petName);
        boolean running = true;
        while (running) {
            System.out.println("\nWhat would you like to do with " + pet.petName + "?");
            System.out.println("1. Feed " + pet.petName);
            System.out.println("2. Play with " + pet.petName);
            System.out.println("3. Check " + pet.petName + "'s status");
            System.out.println("4. Quit");
            System.out.print("Enter your choice (1-4): ");
            int choice = scanner.nextInt();
            switch (choice) {
                case 1:
                    pet.feedPet();
                    break;
                case 2:
                    pet.playWithPet();
                    break;
                case 3:
                    pet.checkStatus();
                    break;
                case 4:
                    running = false;
                    break;
                default:
                    System.out.println("Invalid choice. Please enter a number between 1 and 4.");
            }
```

```
        }
        System.out.println("Thank you for playing with " + pet.petName + "!");
        scanner.close();
    }
}
```

40. Maze Generator and Solver

Maze Generator (Depth-First Search)

```
import java.util.*;
public class MazeGenerator {
    private static final char WALL = '#';
    private static final char PASSAGE = ' ';
    private static final int[] DIRECTION_X = {1, -1, 0, 0}; // Right, Left, Down, Up
    private static final int[] DIRECTION_Y = {0, 0, 1, -1};
    private char[][] maze;
    private int width;
    private int height;
    private Random random;
    public MazeGenerator(int width, int height) {
        this.width = width;
        this.height = height;
        this.maze = new char[height][width];
        this.random = new Random();
        initializeMaze();
    }
    private void initializeMaze() {
        // Initialize maze with walls
        for (int i = 0; i < height; i++) {
            Arrays.fill(maze[i], WALL);
        }
        // Create passages using DFS
        generateMazeDFS(1, 1);
    }
    private void generateMazeDFS(int x, int y) {
        maze[y][x] = PASSAGE; // Mark current cell as passage
        List<Integer> directions = Arrays.asList(0, 1, 2, 3);
        Collections.shuffle(directions, random);
        for (int dir : directions) {
            int newX = x + DIRECTION_X[dir] * 2;
```

```
        int newY = y + DIRECTION_Y[dir] * 2;
        if (newX > 0 && newX < width - 1 && newY > 0 && newY < height - 1 &&
maze[newY][newX] == WALL) {
          maze[y + DIRECTION_Y[dir]][x + DIRECTION_X[dir]] = PASSAGE;
          generateMazeDFS(newX, newY);
        }
      }
    }
    public void displayMaze() {
      for (char[] row : maze) {
        System.out.println(String.valueOf(row));
      }
    }
    public static void main(String[] args) {
      MazeGenerator mazeGenerator = new MazeGenerator(21, 11);
      System.out.println("Generated Maze:");
      mazeGenerator.displayMaze();
    }
}
```

Maze Solver (Breadth-First Search)

```
import java.util.*;
public class MazeSolver {
    private static final char WALL = '#';
    private static final char PASSAGE = ' ';
    private static final char START = 'S';
    private static final char GOAL = 'G';
    private static final int[] DIRECTION_X = {1, -1, 0, 0}; // Right, Left, Down, Up
    private static final int[] DIRECTION_Y = {0, 0, 1, -1};
    private char[][] maze;
    private int width;
    private int height;
    public MazeSolver(char[][] maze) {
      this.maze = maze;
```

```
        this.height = maze.length;
        this.width = maze[0].length;
    }
    public List<int[]> solveMaze() {
        Queue<int[]> queue = new LinkedList<>();
        boolean[][] visited = new boolean[height][width];
        // Find start position
        int startX = -1, startY = -1;
        for (int y = 0; y < height; y++) {
            for (int x = 0; x < width; x++) {
                if (maze[y][x] == START) {
                    startX = x;
                    startY = y;
                    break;
                }
            }
        }
        queue.offer(new int[]{startX, startY});
        visited[startY][startX] = true;
        while (!queue.isEmpty()) {
            int[] current = queue.poll();
            int x = current[0];
            int y = current[1];
            if (maze[y][x] == GOAL) {
                return reconstructPath(current);
            }
            for (int dir = 0; dir < 4; dir++) {
                int newX = x + DIRECTION_X[dir];
                int newY = y + DIRECTION_Y[dir];
                if (isValidMove(newX, newY) && !visited[newY][newX]) {
                    queue.offer(new int[]{newX, newY});
                    visited[newY][newX] = true;
                }
```

```
            }
        }
        return Collections.emptyList();
    }
    private boolean isValidMove(int x, int y) {
        return x >= 0 && x < width && y >= 0 && y < height && maze[y][x] != WALL;
    }
    private List<int[]> reconstructPath(int[] goal) {
        List<int[]> path = new ArrayList<>();
        int x = goal[0];
        int y = goal[1];
        while (maze[y][x] != START) {
            path.add(new int[]{x, y});
            for (int dir = 0; dir < 4; dir++) {
                int newX = x + DIRECTION_X[dir];
                int newY = y + DIRECTION_Y[dir];
                if (isValidMove(newX, newY) && maze[newY][newX] == PASSAGE) {
                    x = newX;
                    y = newY;
                    break;
                }
            }
        }
        path.add(new int[]{x, y});
        Collections.reverse(path);
        return path;
    }
    public static void main(String[] args) {
        char[][] maze = {
            {'#', '#', '#', '#', '#', '#', '#', '#', '#', '#'},
            {'#', 'S', ' ', ' ', ' ', '#', ' ', ' ', ' ', '#'},
            {'#', '#', '#', '#', ' ', '#', ' ', '#', ' ', '#'},
            {'#', ' ', ' ', ' ', ' ', ' ', ' ', '#', ' ', '#'},
```

```
            {'#', ' ', '#', '#', '#', '#', ' ', '#', ' ', '#'},
            {'#', ' ', ' ', ' ', ' ', ' ', ' ', ' ', ' ', '#'},
            {'#', '#', '#', '#', '#', '#', '#', '#', '#', '#'},
            {'#', ' ', ' ', ' ', ' ', ' ', ' ', ' ', 'G', '#'},
            {'#', '#', '#', '#', '#', '#', '#', '#', '#', '#'}
        };
        MazeSolver mazeSolver = new MazeSolver(maze);
        List<int[]> path = mazeSolver.solveMaze();
        System.out.println("Maze Solution:");
        for (int[] step : path) {
            int x = step[0];
            int y = step[1];
            maze[y][x] = '.';
        }
        for (char[] row : maze) {
            System.out.println(String.valueOf(row));
        }
    }
}
```

41. Math Quiz Game

```
import java.util.Random;
import java.util.Scanner;
public class MathQuizGame {
    private static final int NUM_QUESTIONS = 5; // Number of questions in the quiz
    private Random random = new Random();
    private Scanner scanner = new Scanner(System.in);
    public void startGame() {
        System.out.println("Welcome to the Math Quiz Game!");
        System.out.println("You will be asked " + NUM_QUESTIONS + " arithmetic questions.");
        int correctAnswers = 0;
        for (int i = 1; i <= NUM_QUESTIONS; i++) {
            System.out.println("\nQuestion " + i + ":");
            if (askQuestion()) {
                correctAnswers++;
                System.out.println("Correct!\n");
            } else {
                System.out.println("Incorrect. The correct answer was " + getCorrectAnswer() + "\n");
            }
        }
        System.out.println("Quiz completed!");
        System.out.println("You answered " + correctAnswers + " out of " + NUM_QUESTIONS
+ " questions correctly.");
        scanner.close();
    }
    private boolean askQuestion() {
        int num1 = random.nextInt(20) + 1; // Random number between 1 and 20
        int num2 = random.nextInt(20) + 1; // Random number between 1 and 20
        int operation = random.nextInt(3); // 0: addition, 1: subtraction, 2: multiplication
        switch (operation) {
            case 0:
                System.out.println(num1 + " + " + num2 + " = ?");
                return getUserAnswer() == num1 + num2;
```

```
            case 1:
                System.out.println(num1 + " - " + num2 + " = ?");
                return getUserAnswer() == num1 - num2;
            case 2:
                System.out.println(num1 + " * " + num2 + " = ?");
                return getUserAnswer() == num1 * num2;
            default:
                return false;
        }
    }
    private int getUserAnswer() {
        System.out.print("Enter your answer: ");
        while (!scanner.hasNextInt()) {
            System.out.print("Please enter a valid integer: ");
            scanner.next(); // Consume invalid input
        }
        return scanner.nextInt();
    }
    private int getCorrectAnswer() {
        int num1 = random.nextInt(20) + 1;
        int num2 = random.nextInt(20) + 1;
        int operation = random.nextInt(3);
        switch (operation) {
            case 0:
                return num1 + num2;
            case 1:
                return num1 - num2;
            case 2:
                return num1 * num2;
            default:
                return 0;
        }
    }
```

```
    public static void main(String[] args) {
        MathQuizGame game = new MathQuizGame();
        game.startGame();
    }
}
```

42. Lunar Lander Game

```
import java.util.Scanner;
public class LunarLanderGame {
   private static final double GRAVITY = 1.62; // Moon's gravity (m/s^2)
   private static final double SAFE_LANDING_SPEED = 4.0; // Safe landing speed (m/s)
   private double altitude; // Altitude above moon's surface (m)
   private double velocity; // Velocity of the lander (m/s)
   private double fuel; // Fuel remaining in the lander (units)
   private boolean landed; // Flag to indicate if the lander has landed
   public LunarLanderGame(double altitude, double velocity, double fuel) {
      this.altitude = altitude;
      this.velocity = velocity;
      this.fuel = fuel;
      this.landed = false;
   }
   public void playGame() {
      Scanner scanner = new Scanner(System.in);
      System.out.println("Welcome to Lunar Lander Game!");
      System.out.println("Your goal is to land the spacecraft safely on the moon's surface.");
      System.out.println("Use 't' to ignite the thrusters and control the descent.");
      while (!landed) {
         displayStatus();
         if (altitude <= 0) {
            // Lander has landed
            landed = true;
            System.out.println("Congratulations! You have safely landed on the moon!");
            break;
         }
         System.out.print("Enter 't' to ignite thrusters: ");
         String input = scanner.nextLine().trim().toLowerCase();
         if (input.equals("t")) {
            double thrust = calculateThrust();
            velocity += (GRAVITY - thrust);
```

```
            altitude -= velocity;
            fuel -= thrust;
            if (fuel < 0) {
                fuel = 0;
            }
        } else {
            System.out.println("Invalid input. Press 't' to ignite thrusters.");
        }
        // Check for crash condition
        if (velocity >= SAFE_LANDING_SPEED) {
            System.out.println("Lander crashed! Game over.");
            break;
        }
    }
    scanner.close();
}
private void displayStatus() {
    System.out.println("\nCurrent Altitude: " + altitude + " m");
    System.out.println("Current Velocity: " + velocity + " m/s");
    System.out.println("Fuel Remaining: " + fuel + " units");
}
private double calculateThrust() {
    Scanner scanner = new Scanner(System.in);
    System.out.print("Enter thrust level (0 - " + fuel + " units): ");
    while (true) {
        if (scanner.hasNextDouble()) {
            double thrust = scanner.nextDouble();
            if (thrust >= 0 && thrust <= fuel) {
                return thrust;
            }
        }
        System.out.print("Invalid thrust level. Enter a valid number: ");
        scanner.nextLine(); // Consume invalid input
```

```
        }
    }
    public static void main(String[] args) {
        double initialAltitude = 1000.0; // Initial altitude above moon's surface (m)
        double initialVelocity = 0.0; // Initial velocity of the lander (m/s)
        double initialFuel = 100.0; // Initial fuel amount (units)
        LunarLanderGame game = new LunarLanderGame(initialAltitude, initialVelocity,
initialFuel);
        game.playGame();
    }
}
```

43. Target Shooting Game

```
import java.util.Random;
import java.util.Scanner;
public class TargetShootingGame {
    private static final int MAX_BULLETS = 10; // Maximum number of bullets
    private static final int MAX_TARGET_POSITION = 10; // Maximum target position
    private int bullets; // Number of bullets remaining
    private int targetPosition; // Current position of the target
    private Random random = new Random();
    private Scanner scanner = new Scanner(System.in);
    public TargetShootingGame() {
        this.bullets = MAX_BULLETS;
        this.targetPosition = random.nextInt(MAX_TARGET_POSITION) + 1; // Random initial
position (1 to 10)
    }
    public void playGame() {
        System.out.println("Welcome to Target Shooting Game!");
        System.out.println("Try to hit the target as many times as you can with " +
MAX_BULLETS + " bullets.");
        while (bullets > 0) {
            System.out.println("\nCurrent target position: " + targetPosition);
            System.out.println("Bullets remaining: " + bullets);
            System.out.print("Enter your shot position (1 to 10) or 0 to quit: ");
            int shotPosition = scanner.nextInt();
            if (shotPosition == 0) {
                break; // Exit the game
            }
            if (shotPosition < 1 || shotPosition > 10) {
                System.out.println("Invalid shot position. Please enter a number between 1 and 10.");
                continue;
            }
            if (shotPosition == targetPosition) {
                System.out.println("Hit! You scored a point.");
```

```
        } else {
            System.out.println("Miss!");
        }
        targetPosition = random.nextInt(MAX_TARGET_POSITION) + 1; // Randomize target
position
        bullets--;
      }
      System.out.println("\nGame over!");
      System.out.println("You scored " + (MAX_BULLETS - bullets) + " points.");
      scanner.close();
   }
   public static void main(String[] args) {
      TargetShootingGame game = new TargetShootingGame();
      game.playGame();
   }
}
```

44. Weather Simulation Game

```
import java.util.Random;
import java.util.Scanner;
public class WeatherSimulationGame {
    private static final int NUM_DAYS = 7; // Number of days in the simulation
    private Random random = new Random();
    private Scanner scanner = new Scanner(System.in);
    public void playGame() {
        System.out.println("Welcome to Weather Simulation Game!");
        System.out.println("You will receive the weather forecast for the next " + NUM_DAYS + "
days.");
        for (int day = 1; day <= NUM_DAYS; day++) {
            String weatherForecast = generateWeatherForecast();
            System.out.println("\nDay " + day + " Weather Forecast: " + weatherForecast);
            System.out.print("Do you want to (1) go outside or (2) stay indoors? Enter your choice:
");
            int choice = scanner.nextInt();
            if (choice == 1) {
                if (isGoodWeather(weatherForecast)) {
                    System.out.println("You enjoyed a nice day outside!");
                } else {
                    System.out.println("Oops! Bad weather. You should have stayed indoors.");
                }
            } else if (choice == 2) {
                System.out.println("You stayed indoors.");
            } else {
                System.out.println("Invalid choice. Please enter 1 or 2.");
            }
        }
        System.out.println("\nWeather simulation completed for " + NUM_DAYS + " days.");
        scanner.close();
    }
    private String generateWeatherForecast() {
```

```
        String[] weatherConditions = {"Sunny", "Cloudy", "Rainy", "Stormy"};
        int index = random.nextInt(weatherConditions.length);
        return weatherConditions[index];
    }
    private boolean isGoodWeather(String weatherForecast) {
        return weatherForecast.equals("Sunny") || weatherForecast.equals("Cloudy");
    }
    public static void main(String[] args) {
        WeatherSimulationGame game = new WeatherSimulationGame();
        game.playGame();
    }
}
```

45. Simple Music Player Game

```
import java.util.ArrayList;
import java.util.List;
import java.util.Random;
import java.util.Scanner;
public class MusicPlayerGame {
    private List<String> playlist = new ArrayList<>();
    private int currentTrackIndex = -1;
    private boolean playing = false;
    private Random random = new Random();
    private Scanner scanner = new Scanner(System.in);
    public void addSong(String songName) {
        playlist.add(songName);
    }
    public void startGame() {
        System.out.println("Welcome to the Simple Music Player Game!");
        System.out.println("You can manage your playlist and play songs.");
        while (true) {
            displayMenu();
            int choice = scanner.nextInt();
            switch (choice) {
                case 1:
                    addSongToPlaylist();
                    break;
                case 2:
                    playNextSong();
                    break;
                case 3:
                    showPlaylist();
                    break;
                case 4:
                    togglePlayPause();
                    break;
```

```
            case 5:
                System.out.println("Exiting the game. Goodbye!");
                scanner.close();
                return;
            default:
                System.out.println("Invalid choice. Please try again.");
        }
    }
}
private void displayMenu() {
    System.out.println("\nMenu:");
    System.out.println("1. Add a song to the playlist");
    System.out.println("2. Play next song");
    System.out.println("3. Show current playlist");
    System.out.println("4. Toggle play/pause");
    System.out.println("5. Exit");
    System.out.print("Enter your choice: ");
}
private void addSongToPlaylist() {
    System.out.print("Enter the name of the song to add: ");
    scanner.nextLine(); // Consume newline
    String songName = scanner.nextLine();
    playlist.add(songName);
    System.out.println(songName + " added to the playlist.");
}
private void playNextSong() {
    if (playlist.isEmpty()) {
        System.out.println("Playlist is empty. Add songs to play.");
        return;
    }
    if (!playing) {
        currentTrackIndex = random.nextInt(playlist.size());
        playing = true;
```

```
            System.out.println("Playing: " + playlist.get(currentTrackIndex));
        } else {
            System.out.println("Skipping to next song.");
            currentTrackIndex = (currentTrackIndex + 1) % playlist.size();
            System.out.println("Playing: " + playlist.get(currentTrackIndex));
        }
    }
    private void showPlaylist() {
        if (playlist.isEmpty()) {
            System.out.println("Playlist is empty.");
        } else {
            System.out.println("Current Playlist:");
            for (String song : playlist) {
                System.out.println("- " + song);
            }
        }
    }
    private void togglePlayPause() {
        if (playlist.isEmpty()) {
            System.out.println("Playlist is empty. Add songs to play.");
            return;
        }       if (playing) {
            System.out.println("Pausing...");
            playing = false;
        } else {
            System.out.println("Resuming...");
            playing = true;
            System.out.println("Playing: " + playlist.get(currentTrackIndex));
        }   }
    public static void main(String[] args) {
        MusicPlayerGame game = new MusicPlayerGame();
        game.startGame();
    }}
```

46. Word Scramble Game

```
import java.util.ArrayList;
import java.util.List;
import java.util.Random;
import java.util.Scanner;
public class WordScrambleGame {
  private static final int MAX_SCORE = 10; // Maximum score achievable
  private static final int TIME_LIMIT_SECONDS = 30; // Time limit for each word in
seconds
  private List<String> wordList = new ArrayList<>();
  private Random random = new Random();
  private Scanner scanner = new Scanner(System.in);
  private int score = 0;
  public WordScrambleGame() {
    initializeWordList();
  }
  private void initializeWordList() {
    wordList.add("programming");
    wordList.add("java");
    wordList.add("computer");
    wordList.add("algorithm");
    wordList.add("software");
    // Add more words as desired
  }
  public void playGame() {
    System.out.println("Welcome to Word Scramble Game!");
    System.out.println("Unscramble the given word within " + TIME_LIMIT_SECONDS
+ " seconds to earn points.");
    System.out.println("Enter 'q' to quit the game.");
    while (score < MAX_SCORE) {
      String scrambledWord = scrambleWord();
      System.out.println("Scrambled Word: " + scrambledWord);
```

```
            long startTime = System.currentTimeMillis();
            System.out.print("Your answer: ");
            String playerAnswer = scanner.nextLine().trim().toLowerCase();
            if (playerAnswer.equals("q")) {
                break; // Quit the game
            }
            long endTime = System.currentTimeMillis();
            int elapsedTimeSeconds = (int) ((endTime - startTime) / 1000);
            if (elapsedTimeSeconds > TIME_LIMIT_SECONDS) {
                System.out.println("Time's up! The correct answer was: " +
    unscrambleWord(scrambledWord));
            } else {
                if (playerAnswer.equals(unscrambleWord(scrambledWord))) {
                    System.out.println("Correct! You earned 1 point.");
                    score++;
                } else {
                    System.out.println("Incorrect. Try again!");
                }
            }
        }
        System.out.println("\nGame over!");
        System.out.println("Final Score: " + score + " / " + MAX_SCORE);
        scanner.close();
    }
    private String scrambleWord() {
        String word = wordList.get(random.nextInt(wordList.size()));
        char[] characters = word.toCharArray();
        for (int i = characters.length - 1; i > 0; i--) {
            int index = random.nextInt(i + 1);
            // Swap characters
            char temp = characters[index];
            characters[index] = characters[i];
```

```
            characters[i] = temp;
        }
        return new String(characters);
    }
    private String unscrambleWord(String scrambledWord) {
        for (String word : wordList) {
            if (scrambledWord.equals(scrambleWord(word))) {
                return word;
            }
        }
        return ""; // Should never reach here if word is in the list
    }
    public static void main(String[] args) {
        WordScrambleGame game = new WordScrambleGame();
        game.playGame();
    }
}
```

47. Reaction Time Game with Colors

```
import java.awt.Color;
import java.util.Random;
import java.util.Scanner;
public class ReactionTimeGame {
   private static final String[] COLOR_NAMES = {"Red", "Green", "Blue", "Yellow",
"Orange", "Purple"};
   private static final Color[] COLORS = {Color.RED, Color.GREEN, Color.BLUE,
Color.YELLOW, Color.ORANGE, new Color(128, 0, 128)}; // Purple
   private static final int NUM_ROUNDS = 10; // Number of rounds in the game
   private Random random = new Random();
   private Scanner scanner = new Scanner(System.in);
   public void playGame() {
      System.out.println("Welcome to the Reaction Time Game with Colors!");
      System.out.println("Type the name of the color shown in the text as quickly as possible.");
      int totalReactionTime = 0;
      for (int round = 1; round <= NUM_ROUNDS; round++) {
         Color randomColor = COLORS[random.nextInt(COLORS.length)];
         String colorName = COLOR_NAMES[random.nextInt(COLOR_NAMES.length)];
         System.out.print("Round " + round + ": ");
         printColoredText(colorName, randomColor);
         long startTime = System.currentTimeMillis();
         String playerAnswer = scanner.nextLine().trim();
         long endTime = System.currentTimeMillis();
         if (playerAnswer.equalsIgnoreCase(colorName)) {
            int reactionTime = (int) (endTime - startTime);
            System.out.println("Correct! Reaction time: " + reactionTime + " ms");
            totalReactionTime += reactionTime;
         } else {
            System.out.println("Incorrect! The correct color was " + colorName);
         }
      }
      double averageReactionTime = (double) totalReactionTime / NUM_ROUNDS;
```

```
        System.out.println("\nGame Over!");
        System.out.println("Average Reaction Time: " + averageReactionTime + " ms");
        scanner.close();
    }
    private void printColoredText(String text, Color color) {
        String colorCode = String.format("\033[38;2;%d;%d;%dm", color.getRed(),
color.getGreen(), color.getBlue());
        System.out.println(colorCode + text + "\033[0m");
    }
    public static void main(String[] args) {
        ReactionTimeGame game = new ReactionTimeGame();
        game.playGame();
    }
}
```

48. Simple Slot Machine

```
import java.util.Random;
import java.util.Scanner;
public class SlotMachineGame {
    private static final String[] SYMBOLS = {"Cherry", "Orange", "Lemon", "Apple", "Grapes",
"Banana"};
    private static final int[] PAYOUTS = {50, 30, 20, 10, 5, 2}; // Coin payouts for symbol
matches
    private static final int INITIAL_COINS = 100; // Initial number of coins
    private static final int SPIN_COST = 10; // Cost per spin
    private Random random = new Random();
    private Scanner scanner = new Scanner(System.in);
    private int coins;
    public SlotMachineGame() {
        this.coins = INITIAL_COINS;
    }
    public void playGame() {
        System.out.println("Welcome to the Simple Slot Machine Game!");
        System.out.println("Match three symbols to win coins. Each spin costs " + SPIN_COST +
" coins.");
        while (coins >= SPIN_COST) {
            System.out.println("\nCoins: " + coins);
            System.out.print("Press Enter to spin the reels (or 'q' to quit): ");
            String input = scanner.nextLine().trim().toLowerCase();
            if (input.equals("q")) {
                break; // Quit the game
            }
            coins -= SPIN_COST;
            String[] reels = spinReels();
            System.out.println("Reels: " + reels[0] + " | " + reels[1] + " | " + reels[2]);
            int payout = calculatePayout(reels);
            if (payout > 0) {
                coins += payout;
```

```
            System.out.println("Congratulations! You won " + payout + " coins.");
        } else {
            System.out.println("Spin again! No winning combination.");
        }
    }
    System.out.println("\nGame over! Final coins: " + coins);
    scanner.close();
  }
  private String[] spinReels() {
    String[] reels = new String[3];
    for (int i = 0; i < 3; i++) {
      reels[i] = SYMBOLS[random.nextInt(SYMBOLS.length)];
    }
    return reels;
  }
  private int calculatePayout(String[] reels) {
    if (reels[0].equals(reels[1]) && reels[1].equals(reels[2])) {
      for (int i = 0; i < SYMBOLS.length; i++) {
        if (reels[0].equals(SYMBOLS[i])) {
          return PAYOUTS[i] * SPIN_COST;
        }
      }
    }
    return 0; // No winning combination
  }
  public static void main(String[] args) {
    SlotMachineGame game = new SlotMachineGame();
    game.playGame();
  }
}
```

49. Building Blocks Tower Game

```
import java.util.Scanner;
public class TowerBuildingGame {
    private static final int MAX_HEIGHT = 10; // Maximum height of the tower
    private static final int INITIAL_BASE_WIDTH = 3; // Initial width of the tower's base
    private int towerHeight; // Current height of the tower
    private int baseWidth; // Current width of the tower's base
    private Scanner scanner = new Scanner(System.in);
    public TowerBuildingGame() {
        this.towerHeight = 0;
        this.baseWidth = INITIAL_BASE_WIDTH;
    }
    public void playGame() {
        System.out.println("Welcome to the Building Blocks Tower Game!");
        System.out.println("Add blocks to build a tower without making it topple over.");
        System.out.println("Enter 'q' to quit the game.");
        while (towerHeight < MAX_HEIGHT) {
            displayTower();
            System.out.print("Enter number of blocks to add (1-" + baseWidth + "): ");
            String input = scanner.nextLine().trim().toLowerCase();
            if (input.equals("q")) {
                break; // Quit the game
            }
            try {
                int blocksToAdd = Integer.parseInt(input);
                if (blocksToAdd < 1 || blocksToAdd > baseWidth) {
                    System.out.println("Invalid number of blocks. Please enter a number between 1 and
" + baseWidth + ".");
                    continue;
                }
                towerHeight += blocksToAdd;
                baseWidth = Math.min(baseWidth + 1, INITIAL_BASE_WIDTH + towerHeight); //
Increase base width gradually
```

```
        } catch (NumberFormatException e) {
            System.out.println("Invalid input. Please enter a valid number of blocks or 'q' to
quit.");
        }
    }
    if (towerHeight >= MAX_HEIGHT) {
        System.out.println("\nCongratulations! You've built a " + MAX_HEIGHT + "-block
tower!");
    } else {
        System.out.println("\nGame over! Tower height: " + towerHeight);
    }
    scanner.close();
  }
  private void displayTower() {
    System.out.println("\nCurrent Tower (Height: " + towerHeight + "):");
    for (int i = 0; i < towerHeight; i++) {
        for (int j = 0; j < baseWidth; j++) {
            System.out.print("|");
        }
        System.out.println();
    }
  }
  public static void main(String[] args) {
    TowerBuildingGame game = new TowerBuildingGame();
    game.playGame();
  }
}
```

50. Pac-Man Style Maze Game

```
import java.util.Scanner;
public class PacManMazeGame {
   private static final int MAZE_SIZE = 10; // Size of the square maze (MAZE_SIZE x
MAZE_SIZE)
   private static final char EMPTY_CELL = '.';
   private static final char PLAYER_CHAR = 'P';
   private static final char WALL_CHAR = '#';
   private static final char FOOD_CHAR = '*';
   private static final char ENEMY_CHAR = 'E';
   private char[][] maze = new char[MAZE_SIZE][MAZE_SIZE];
   private int playerRow;
   private int playerCol;
   private int foodCount;
   private int enemyCount;
   private Scanner scanner = new Scanner(System.in);
   public PacManMazeGame() {
      initializeMaze();
      placePlayer();
      placeFood();
      placeEnemies();
   }
   private void initializeMaze() {
      for (int row = 0; row < MAZE_SIZE; row++) {
         for (int col = 0; col < MAZE_SIZE; col++) {
            if (row == 0 || row == MAZE_SIZE - 1 || col == 0 || col == MAZE_SIZE - 1) {
               maze[row][col] = WALL_CHAR; // Border walls
            } else {
               maze[row][col] = EMPTY_CELL; // Empty cells
            }
         }
      }
   }
```

```
private void placePlayer() {
    playerRow = MAZE_SIZE / 2;
    playerCol = MAZE_SIZE / 2;
    maze[playerRow][playerCol] = PLAYER_CHAR;
}
private void placeFood() {
    foodCount = MAZE_SIZE * 2; // Place food items based on maze size
    while (foodCount > 0) {
        int row = (int) (Math.random() * MAZE_SIZE);
        int col = (int) (Math.random() * MAZE_SIZE);
        if (maze[row][col] == EMPTY_CELL) {
            maze[row][col] = FOOD_CHAR;
            foodCount--;
        }
    }
}
private void placeEnemies() {
    enemyCount = MAZE_SIZE / 2; // Place enemies based on maze size
    while (enemyCount > 0) {
        int row = (int) (Math.random() * MAZE_SIZE);
        int col = (int) (Math.random() * MAZE_SIZE);
        if (maze[row][col] == EMPTY_CELL) {
            maze[row][col] = ENEMY_CHAR;
            enemyCount--;
        }
    }
}
public void playGame() {
    System.out.println("Welcome to the Pac-Man Style Maze Game!");
    displayMaze();
    while (foodCount > 0) {
        System.out.print("Enter your move (WASD or 'q' to quit): ");
        String move = scanner.next().trim().toLowerCase();
```

```
            if (move.equals("q")) {
                System.out.println("Game over. Thanks for playing!");
                break;
            }
            movePlayer(move);
            displayMaze();
            if (foodCount == 0) {
                System.out.println("Congratulations! You've eaten all the food.");
            }
        }
        scanner.close();
    }
    private void movePlayer(String direction) {
        int newRow = playerRow;
        int newCol = playerCol;
        switch (direction) {
            case "w":
                newRow--;
                break;
            case "a":
                newCol--;
                break;
            case "s":
                newRow++;
                break;
            case "d":
                newCol++;
                break;
            default:
                System.out.println("Invalid move. Use WASD to move or 'q' to quit.");
                return;
        }
```

```
        if (maze[newRow][newCol] == EMPTY_CELL || maze[newRow][newCol] ==
FOOD_CHAR) {
            if (maze[newRow][newCol] == FOOD_CHAR) {
                foodCount--;
            }
            maze[playerRow][playerCol] = EMPTY_CELL;
            maze[newRow][newCol] = PLAYER_CHAR;
            playerRow = newRow;
            playerCol = newCol;
        } else if (maze[newRow][newCol] == ENEMY_CHAR) {
            System.out.println("Game over! You've been caught by an enemy.");
            foodCount = 0; // Game ends
        } else {
            System.out.println("Invalid move. Cannot move through walls.");
        }
    }
    private void displayMaze() {
        System.out.println("\nCurrent Maze:");
        for (int row = 0; row < MAZE_SIZE; row++) {
            for (int col = 0; col < MAZE_SIZE; col++) {
                System.out.print(maze[row][col] + " ");
            }
            System.out.println();
        }
    }
    public static void main(String[] args) {
        PacManMazeGame game = new PacManMazeGame();
        game.playGame();
    }
}
```

51. Breakout with Power-ups

```
import javax.swing.*;
import java.awt.*;
import java.awt.event.*;
public class BreakoutGame extends JPanel implements ActionListener {
    private static final int WIDTH = 800;
    private static final int HEIGHT = 600;
    private static final int PADDLE_WIDTH = 100;
    private static final int PADDLE_HEIGHT = 20;
    private static final int BALL_DIAMETER = 20;
    private static final int BLOCK_WIDTH = 60;
    private static final int BLOCK_HEIGHT = 30;
    private static final int NUM_BLOCKS = 50;
    private static final int PADDLE_SPEED = 10;
    private static final int BALL_SPEED = 5;
    private boolean gameRunning = true;
    private Timer timer;
    private int paddleX = WIDTH / 2 - PADDLE_WIDTH / 2;
    private int ballX = WIDTH / 2 - BALL_DIAMETER / 2;
    private int ballY = HEIGHT - 100;
    private int ballDX = BALL_SPEED;
    private int ballDY = -BALL_SPEED;
    private boolean paddleLeft = false;
    private boolean paddleRight = false;
    private Rectangle paddle;
    private Rectangle ball;
    private Rectangle[] blocks;
    private boolean[] blockDestroyed;
    private boolean paddleGunActive = false;
    private boolean multiBallActive = false;
    private int numBalls = 1;
    public BreakoutGame() {
        setPreferredSize(new Dimension(WIDTH, HEIGHT));
```

```
    setBackground(Color.BLACK);
    setFocusable(true);
    paddle = new Rectangle(paddleX, HEIGHT - PADDLE_HEIGHT - 10,
PADDLE_WIDTH, PADDLE_HEIGHT);
    ball = new Rectangle(ballX, ballY, BALL_DIAMETER, BALL_DIAMETER);
    blocks = new Rectangle[NUM_BLOCKS];
    blockDestroyed = new boolean[NUM_BLOCKS];
    // Initialize blocks
    int blockIndex = 0;
    int xOffset = 50;
    int yOffset = 50;
    for (int row = 0; row < 5; row++) {
      for (int col = 0; col < 10; col++) {
        blocks[blockIndex] = new Rectangle(xOffset + col * (BLOCK_WIDTH + 10),
            yOffset + row * (BLOCK_HEIGHT + 10), BLOCK_WIDTH,
BLOCK_HEIGHT);
        blockDestroyed[blockIndex] = false;
        blockIndex++;
      }
    }
    addKeyListener(new KeyAdapter() {
      @Override
      public void keyPressed(KeyEvent e) {
        int key = e.getKeyCode();
        if (key == KeyEvent.VK_LEFT) {
          paddleLeft = true;
        }
        if (key == KeyEvent.VK_RIGHT) {
          paddleRight = true;
        }
      }
      @Override
      public void keyReleased(KeyEvent e) {
```

```
            int key = e.getKeyCode();
            if (key == KeyEvent.VK_LEFT) {
               paddleLeft = false;
            }
            if (key == KeyEvent.VK_RIGHT) {
               paddleRight = false;
            }
         }
      });
      timer = new Timer(1000 / 60, this);
      timer.start();
   }
   @Override
   public void paintComponent(Graphics g) {
      super.paintComponent(g);
      Graphics2D g2d = (Graphics2D) g;
      g2d.setRenderingHint(RenderingHints.KEY_ANTIALIASING,
RenderingHints.VALUE_ANTIALIAS_ON);
      // Draw paddle
      g2d.setColor(Color.WHITE);
      g2d.fill(paddle);
      // Draw ball
      g2d.setColor(Color.RED);
      g2d.fill(ball);
      // Draw blocks
      for (int i = 0; i < blocks.length; i++) {
         if (!blockDestroyed[i]) {
            g2d.setColor(Color.BLUE);
            g2d.fill(blocks[i]);
         }
      }
   }
   @Override
```

```
public void actionPerformed(ActionEvent e) {
    if (gameRunning) {
        movePaddle();
        moveBall();
        checkCollisions();
        repaint();
    }
}
private void movePaddle() {
    if (paddleLeft && paddleX > 0) {
        paddleX -= PADDLE_SPEED;
    }
    if (paddleRight && paddleX < WIDTH - PADDLE_WIDTH) {
        paddleX += PADDLE_SPEED;
    }
    paddle.setLocation(paddleX, HEIGHT - PADDLE_HEIGHT - 10);
}
private void moveBall() {
    ball.x += ballDX;
    ball.y += ballDY;
    // Bounce off walls
    if (ball.x <= 0 || ball.x + BALL_DIAMETER >= WIDTH) {
        ballDX = -ballDX;
    }
    if (ball.y <= 0) {
        ballDY = -ballDY;
    }
    // Check paddle collision
    if (ball.intersects(paddle)) {
        ballDY = -ballDY;
    }
    // Check block collision
    for (int i = 0; i < blocks.length; i++) {
```

```
            if (!blockDestroyed[i] && ball.intersects(blocks[i])) {
                blockDestroyed[i] = true;
                ballDY = -ballDY;
            }
        }
        // Check ball out of bounds
        if (ball.y + BALL_DIAMETER >= HEIGHT) {
            gameRunning = false;
            JOptionPane.showMessageDialog(this, "Game Over", "Game Over",
JOptionPane.INFORMATION_MESSAGE);
        }
    }
    private void checkCollisions() {
        // TODO: Implement collision detection with power-ups and block destruction
    }
    public static void main(String[] args) {
        JFrame frame = new JFrame("Breakout with Power-ups");
        BreakoutGame game = new BreakoutGame();
        frame.add(game);
        frame.pack();
        frame.setDefaultCloseOperation(JFrame.EXIT_ON_CLOSE);
        frame.setLocationRelativeTo(null);
        frame.setVisible(true);
    }
}
```

52. Fishing Game

```
import java.util.Scanner;
import java.util.Random;
public class FishingGame {
  private static final int MAX_DIFFICULTY = 5; // Maximum difficulty level
  private static final int SUCCESS_THRESHOLD = 3; // Minimum dice roll for successful
catch
  public static void main(String[] args) {
    Scanner scanner = new Scanner(System.in);
    Random random = new Random();
    System.out.println("Welcome to the Fishing Game!");
    int totalScore = 0;
    boolean continueFishing = true;
    while (continueFishing) {
      System.out.println("\nChoose a fish to catch:");
      System.out.println("1. Small Fish (Difficulty 1)");
      System.out.println("2. Medium Fish (Difficulty 3)");
      System.out.println("3. Large Fish (Difficulty 5)");
      System.out.println("4. Quit");
      System.out.print("Enter your choice: ");
      int choice = scanner.nextInt();
      if (choice == 4) {
        System.out.println("Thanks for playing! Your total score is: " + totalScore);
        break;
      }
      int difficulty = getDifficulty(choice);
      if (difficulty == -1) {
        System.out.println("Invalid choice. Please try again.");
        continue;
      }
      System.out.println("Fishing...");
      int diceRoll = random.nextInt(MAX_DIFFICULTY) + 1; // Roll a dice from 1 to
MAX_DIFFICULTY
```

```
            if (diceRoll >= SUCCESS_THRESHOLD && diceRoll <= difficulty) {
                System.out.println("Congratulations! You caught the fish!");
                totalScore += difficulty;
            } else {
                System.out.println("Oh no! The fish got away...");
            }
        }
        scanner.close();
    }
    // Helper method to get fish difficulty based on user choice
    private static int getDifficulty(int choice) {
        switch (choice) {
            case 1:
                return 1; // Small Fish (Difficulty 1)
            case 2:
                return 3; // Medium Fish (Difficulty 3)
            case 3:
                return 5; // Large Fish (Difficulty 5)
            default:
                return -1; // Invalid choice
        }
    }
}
```

53. Minesweeper Game

```
import java.util.*;
public class MinesweeperGame {
    private static final int BOARD_SIZE = 8;
    private static final int NUM_MINES = 10;
    private static final char UNCOVERED = '-';
    private static final char COVERED = '#';
    private static final char MINE = '*';
    private char[][] board;
    private boolean[][] isMine;
    private boolean[][] uncovered;
    private Random random;
    private Scanner scanner;
    public MinesweeperGame() {
        board = new char[BOARD_SIZE][BOARD_SIZE];
        isMine = new boolean[BOARD_SIZE][BOARD_SIZE];
        uncovered = new boolean[BOARD_SIZE][BOARD_SIZE];
        random = new Random();
        scanner = new Scanner(System.in);
    }
    public void play() {
        initializeBoard();
        displayBoard();
        while (true) {
            System.out.print("Enter row and column (e.g., '0 0') to uncover: ");
            int row = scanner.nextInt();
            int col = scanner.nextInt();
            if (row < 0 || row >= BOARD_SIZE || col < 0 || col >= BOARD_SIZE) {
                System.out.println("Invalid input. Please try again.");
                continue;
            }
            if (uncoverTile(row, col)) {
                displayBoard();
```

```
                System.out.println("Game over! You uncovered a mine. Try again!");
                break;
            }
            if (checkWin()) {
                displayBoard();
                System.out.println("Congratulations! You've uncovered all safe tiles!");
                break;
            }
            displayBoard();
        }
        scanner.close();
    }
    private void initializeBoard() {
        // Initialize board with covered tiles
        for (int i = 0; i < BOARD_SIZE; i++) {
            for (int j = 0; j < BOARD_SIZE; j++) {
                board[i][j] = COVERED;
            }
        }
        // Place mines randomly on the board
        int placedMines = 0;
        while (placedMines < NUM_MINES) {
            int row = random.nextInt(BOARD_SIZE);
            int col = random.nextInt(BOARD_SIZE);
            if (!isMine[row][col]) {
                isMine[row][col] = true;
                placedMines++;
            }
        }
    }
    private void displayBoard() {
        System.out.println("  0 1 2 3 4 5 6 7");
        for (int i = 0; i < BOARD_SIZE; i++) {
```

```
        System.out.print(i + "  ");
        for (int j = 0; j < BOARD_SIZE; j++) {
          if (uncovered[i][j]) {
            System.out.print(board[i][j] + " ");
          } else {
            System.out.print(COVERED + " ");
          }
        }
        System.out.println();
      }
    }
  private boolean uncoverTile(int row, int col) {
    if (uncovered[row][col]) {
      System.out.println("Tile already uncovered. Choose another tile.");
      return false;
    }
    uncovered[row][col] = true;
    if (isMine[row][col]) {
      board[row][col] = MINE;
      return true;
    }
    // Calculate adjacent mines
    int numMines = countAdjacentMines(row, col);
    board[row][col] = (char) (numMines + '0'); // Convert int to char
    // If no adjacent mines, recursively uncover neighbors
    if (numMines == 0) {
      for (int dr = -1; dr <= 1; dr++) {
        for (int dc = -1; dc <= 1; dc++) {
          int newRow = row + dr;
          int newCol = col + dc;
          if (newRow >= 0 && newRow < BOARD_SIZE && newCol >= 0 && newCol <
BOARD_SIZE) {
            if (!uncovered[newRow][newCol]) {
```

```
                    uncoverTile(newRow, newCol);
                }
            }
        }
    }
    }
    return false;
}
private int countAdjacentMines(int row, int col) {
    int count = 0;
    for (int dr = -1; dr <= 1; dr++) {
        for (int dc = -1; dc <= 1; dc++) {
            int newRow = row + dr;
            int newCol = col + dc;
            if (newRow >= 0 && newRow < BOARD_SIZE && newCol >= 0 && newCol <
BOARD_SIZE) {
                if (isMine[newRow][newCol]) {
                    count++;
                }
            }
        }
    }
    return count;
}
private boolean checkWin() {
    for (int i = 0; i < BOARD_SIZE; i++) {
        for (int j = 0; j < BOARD_SIZE; j++) {
            if (!uncovered[i][j] && !isMine[i][j]) {
                return false; // Found a covered safe tile
            }
        }
    }
    return true; // All safe tiles are uncovered
```

```
    }

    public static void main(String[] args) {
        MinesweeperGame game = new MinesweeperGame();
        game.play();
    }
}
```

54. Hangman with ASCII Art

```
import java.util.*;
public class HangmanGame {
    private static final String[] WORDS = { "java", "programming", "computer", "algorithm",
"software" };
    private static final String[] HANGMAN_ART = {
        " +---+\n |   |\n     |\n     |\n     |\n     |\n=========",
        " +---+\n |   |\n O   |\n     |\n     |\n     |\n=========",
        " +---+\n |   |\n O   |\n |   |\n     |\n     |\n=========",
        " +---+\n |   |\n O   |\n /|  |\n     |\n     |\n=========",
        " +---+\n |   |\n O   |\n /|\\ |\n     |\n     |\n=========",
        " +---+\n |   |\n O   |\n /|\\ |\n /   |\n     |\n=========",
        " +---+\n |   |\n O   |\n /|\\ |\n / \\ |\n     |\n========="
    };
    private String secretWord;
    private StringBuilder guessedLetters;
    private int incorrectAttempts;
    private Random random;
    private Scanner scanner;
    public HangmanGame() {
        random = new Random();
        scanner = new Scanner(System.in);
    }
    public void play() {
        secretWord = selectRandomWord();
        guessedLetters = new StringBuilder(secretWord.length());
        for (int i = 0; i < secretWord.length(); i++) {
            guessedLetters.append('_');
        }
        incorrectAttempts = 0;
        System.out.println("Welcome to Hangman!");
        System.out.println(HANGMAN_ART[0]); // Initial empty hangman
        while (incorrectAttempts < HANGMAN_ART.length - 1) {
```

```
            System.out.println("Word: " + guessedLetters.toString());
            System.out.print("Guess a letter: ");
            String guess = scanner.nextLine().toLowerCase();
            if (guess.length() != 1 || !Character.isLetter(guess.charAt(0))) {
                System.out.println("Invalid input. Please enter a single letter.");
                continue;
            }
            if (updateGuessedLetters(guess.charAt(0))) {
                System.out.println("Correct guess!");
            } else {
                incorrectAttempts++;
                System.out.println("Incorrect guess!");
                System.out.println(HANGMAN_ART[incorrectAttempts]);
                if (incorrectAttempts == HANGMAN_ART.length - 1) {
                    System.out.println("You've run out of attempts! The word was: " + secretWord);
                    break;
                }
            }
            if (guessedLetters.toString().equals(secretWord)) {
                System.out.println("Congratulations! You guessed the word: " + secretWord);
                break;
            }
        }
        scanner.close();
    }
    private String selectRandomWord() {
        return WORDS[random.nextInt(WORDS.length)];
    }
    private boolean updateGuessedLetters(char guess) {
        boolean correctGuess = false;
        for (int i = 0; i < secretWord.length(); i++) {
            if (secretWord.charAt(i) == guess) {
                guessedLetters.setCharAt(i, guess);
```

```
            correctGuess = true;
        }
      }
      return correctGuess;
   }
   public static void main(String[] args) {
      HangmanGame game = new HangmanGame();
      game.play();
   }
}
```

55. Simple Cricket Game

```
import java.util.*;
public class SimpleCricketGame {
    private static final int MAX_OVERS = 5;
    private static final int MAX_BALLS_PER_OVER = 6;
    private String[] teams = { "Team A", "Team B" };
    private int[] scores = { 0, 0 };
    private Random random = new Random();
    private Scanner scanner = new Scanner(System.in);
    public void play() {
        System.out.println("Welcome to the Simple Cricket Game!");
        System.out.println("Teams: " + teams[0] + " vs " + teams[1]);
        System.out.println("Let's play " + MAX_OVERS + " overs match.");
        for (int over = 1; over <= MAX_OVERS; over++) {
            System.out.println("\nOver " + over + " begins!");
            for (int ball = 1; ball <= MAX_BALLS_PER_OVER; ball++) {
                int battingTeam = (over % 2 == 1) ? 0 : 1; // Alternate batting team each over
                int runsScored = simulateBall();
                System.out.println("Ball " + ball + ": " + teams[battingTeam] + " scores " +
runsScored + " run(s).");
                scores[battingTeam] += runsScored;
                if (ball == MAX_BALLS_PER_OVER || over == MAX_OVERS) {
                    // Display score after each over
                    System.out.println("End of Over " + over + " - " + teams[battingTeam] + " total
score: " + scores[battingTeam] + "/" + (over - 1) * MAX_BALLS_PER_OVER + " in " + over +
" overs.");
                    break;
                }
                System.out.println("Current score: " + teams[battingTeam] + " " +
scores[battingTeam] + "/" + (over - 1) * MAX_BALLS_PER_OVER + " in " + over + "
overs.");
                System.out.println("Press Enter to bowl the next ball...");
                scanner.nextLine();
```

```
        }
        // Swap batting teams after each over
        System.out.println("End of Over " + over);
        swapBattingTeams();
      }
      // Determine winner
      int winnerIndex = (scores[0] > scores[1]) ? 0 : 1;
      System.out.println("\nMatch Over!");
      System.out.println("Final Score: " + teams[0] + " " + scores[0] + " - " + teams[1] + " " +
scores[1]);
      System.out.println("Congratulations, " + teams[winnerIndex] + " wins!");
      scanner.close();
   }
   private int simulateBall() {
      // Simulate runs scored on a single ball
      int[] outcomes = { 0, 0, 0, 1, 2, 3, 4, 6 }; // Possible outcomes: dot ball, 0, 1, 2, 3, 4, 6
      int randomIndex = random.nextInt(outcomes.length);
      return outcomes[randomIndex];
   }
   private void swapBattingTeams() {
      // Swap batting teams
      int temp = scores[0];
      scores[0] = scores[1];
      scores[1] = temp;
   }
   public static void main(String[] args) {
      SimpleCricketGame game = new SimpleCricketGame();
      game.play();
   }
}
```

56. Fruit Ninja-style Game

```
import java.util.*;
public class FruitNinjaGame {
    private static final int MAX_FRUITS = 10;
    private static final int FRUIT_TYPES = 3;
    private static final int MIN_SCORE = 1;
    private static final int MAX_SCORE = 5;
    private Random random = new Random();
    private Scanner scanner = new Scanner(System.in);
    private int score = 0;
    public void play() {
        System.out.println("Welcome to Fruit Ninja!");
        System.out.println("Slice the fruits as they appear on the screen.");
        for (int i = 0; i < MAX_FRUITS; i++) {
            System.out.println("\nFruit " + (i + 1) + ":");
            int fruitType = random.nextInt(FRUIT_TYPES); // Randomly select fruit type
            switch (fruitType) {
                case 0:
                    System.out.println("  ___");
                    System.out.println(" /   \\");
                    System.out.println(" | O |");
                    System.out.println(" \\___/");
                    break;
                case 1:
                    System.out.println("  .-^-.");
                    System.out.println(" /_\\/_\\");
                    System.out.println("   | |");
                    break;
                case 2:
                    System.out.println("  ,--.");
                    System.out.println(" (    )");
                    System.out.println("  \\__/");
                    break;
```

```
        }
        System.out.print("Slice the fruit (1 to slice, 0 to skip): ");
        int userAction = scanner.nextInt();
        if (userAction == 1) {
          int fruitScore = random.nextInt(MAX_SCORE - MIN_SCORE + 1) + MIN_SCORE;
          System.out.println("You sliced the fruit! Scored " + fruitScore + " points.");
          score += fruitScore;
        } else {
          System.out.println("Fruit missed!");
        }
      }
      System.out.println("\nGame Over!");
      System.out.println("Total Score: " + score);
      scanner.close();
    }
    public static void main(String[] args) {
      FruitNinjaGame game = new FruitNinjaGame();
      game.play();
    }
}
```

57. Ping Pong Game

```
import javax.swing.*;
import java.awt.*;
import java.awt.event.ActionEvent;
import java.awt.event.ActionListener;
import java.awt.event.KeyEvent;
import java.awt.event.KeyListener;
public class PingPongGame extends JFrame implements ActionListener, KeyListener {
    private static final int WINDOW_WIDTH = 800;
    private static final int WINDOW_HEIGHT = 600;
    private static final int PADDLE_WIDTH = 10;
    private static final int PADDLE_HEIGHT = 100;
    private static final int BALL_SIZE = 20;
    private static final int PADDLE_SPEED = 10;
    private static final int BALL_SPEED = 5;
    private int paddle1Y = WINDOW_HEIGHT / 2 - PADDLE_HEIGHT / 2;
    private int paddle2Y = WINDOW_HEIGHT / 2 - PADDLE_HEIGHT / 2;
    private int ballX = WINDOW_WIDTH / 2 - BALL_SIZE / 2;
    private int ballY = WINDOW_HEIGHT / 2 - BALL_SIZE / 2;
    private int ballXSpeed = BALL_SPEED;
    private int ballYSpeed = BALL_SPEED;
    private int player1Score = 0;
    private int player2Score = 0;
    private boolean upPressed = false;
    private boolean downPressed = false;
    public PingPongGame() {
        setTitle("Ping Pong Game");
        setSize(WINDOW_WIDTH, WINDOW_HEIGHT);
        setDefaultCloseOperation(EXIT_ON_CLOSE);
        setResizable(false);
        Timer timer = new Timer(1000 / 60, this); // 60 FPS
        timer.start();
        addKeyListener(this);
```

```
        setFocusable(true);
    }
    public void paint(Graphics g) {
        super.paint(g);
        // Draw background
        g.setColor(Color.BLACK);
        g.fillRect(0, 0, WINDOW_WIDTH, WINDOW_HEIGHT);
        // Draw paddles
        g.setColor(Color.WHITE);
        g.fillRect(50, paddle1Y, PADDLE_WIDTH, PADDLE_HEIGHT); // Left paddle
        g.fillRect(WINDOW_WIDTH - 50 - PADDLE_WIDTH, paddle2Y, PADDLE_WIDTH,
PADDLE_HEIGHT); // Right paddle
        // Draw ball
        g.fillRect(ballX, ballY, BALL_SIZE, BALL_SIZE);
        // Draw scores
        g.setFont(new Font("Arial", Font.BOLD, 30));
        g.drawString(String.valueOf(player1Score), WINDOW_WIDTH / 2 - 50, 50); // Left
player score
        g.drawString(String.valueOf(player2Score), WINDOW_WIDTH / 2 + 25, 50); // Right
player score
    }
    public void actionPerformed(ActionEvent e) {
        update();
        repaint();
    }
    public void update() {
        // Move paddles
        if (upPressed && paddle1Y > 0) {
            paddle1Y -= PADDLE_SPEED;
        }
        if (downPressed && paddle1Y < WINDOW_HEIGHT - PADDLE_HEIGHT) {
            paddle1Y += PADDLE_SPEED;
        }
```

```
        // AI for the right paddle (computer player)
        int paddle2Center = paddle2Y + PADDLE_HEIGHT / 2;
        if (paddle2Center < ballY) {
            paddle2Y += PADDLE_SPEED;
        } else {
            paddle2Y -= PADDLE_SPEED;
        }
        // Move ball
        ballX += ballXSpeed;
        ballY += ballYSpeed;
        // Ball collision with top/bottom walls
        if (ballY <= 0 || ballY >= WINDOW_HEIGHT - BALL_SIZE) {
            ballYSpeed = -ballYSpeed;
        }
        // Ball collision with paddles
        if (ballX <= 60 && ballY >= paddle1Y && ballY <= paddle1Y + PADDLE_HEIGHT) {
            ballXSpeed = BALL_SPEED;
        }
        if (ballX >= WINDOW_WIDTH - 60 - PADDLE_WIDTH - BALL_SIZE && ballY >=
paddle2Y && ballY <= paddle2Y + PADDLE_HEIGHT) {
            ballXSpeed = -BALL_SPEED;
        }
        // Ball out of bounds (score)
        if (ballX < 0) {
            player2Score++;
            resetBall();
        }
        if (ballX > WINDOW_WIDTH - BALL_SIZE) {
            player1Score++;
            resetBall();
        }
    }
    public void resetBall() {
```

```
        ballX = WINDOW_WIDTH / 2 - BALL_SIZE / 2;
        ballY = WINDOW_HEIGHT / 2 - BALL_SIZE / 2;
        ballXSpeed = BALL_SPEED;
        ballYSpeed = BALL_SPEED;
    }
    public void keyPressed(KeyEvent e) {
        if (e.getKeyCode() == KeyEvent.VK_W) {
            upPressed = true;
        }
        if (e.getKeyCode() == KeyEvent.VK_S) {
            downPressed = true;
        }
    }
    public void keyReleased(KeyEvent e) {
        if (e.getKeyCode() == KeyEvent.VK_W) {
            upPressed = false;
        }
        if (e.getKeyCode() == KeyEvent.VK_S) {
            downPressed = false;
        }
    }
    public void keyTyped(KeyEvent e) {}
    public static void main(String[] args) {
        SwingUtilities.invokeLater(() -> {
            PingPongGame game = new PingPongGame();
            game.setVisible(true);
        });
    }
}
```

58. Guitar Hero-style Rhythm Game

```
import java.util.*;
public class RhythmGame {
    private static final int SCREEN_WIDTH = 40;
    private static final int SCREEN_HEIGHT = 10;
    private static final int NOTE_SPEED = 1; // Speed of falling notes
    private static final int NOTE_INTERVAL = 3; // Interval between new notes (in frames)
    private static final char[] NOTE_SYMBOLS = { 'A', 'S', 'D', 'F' }; // Note symbols
(corresponding to keys)
    private int frameCount = 0;
    private List<Note> notes = new ArrayList<>();
    private Random random = new Random();
    private Scanner scanner = new Scanner(System.in);
    public void play() {
        System.out.println("Welcome to the Rhythm Game!");
        System.out.println("Press corresponding keys when notes reach the bottom.");
        while (true) {
            update();
            display();
            handleInput();
            try {
                Thread.sleep(100); // Adjust game speed (lower value = faster)
            } catch (InterruptedException e) {
                e.printStackTrace();
            }
        }
    }
    private void update() {
        frameCount++;
        // Generate new notes at specified interval
        if (frameCount % NOTE_INTERVAL == 0) {
            int xPos = random.nextInt(SCREEN_WIDTH);
            char noteSymbol = NOTE_SYMBOLS[random.nextInt(NOTE_SYMBOLS.length)];
```

```
        notes.add(new Note(xPos, noteSymbol));
      }
      // Move notes downwards
      Iterator<Note> iterator = notes.iterator();
      while (iterator.hasNext()) {
        Note note = iterator.next();
        note.setY(note.getY() + NOTE_SPEED);
        // Remove notes that have reached the bottom
        if (note.getY() >= SCREEN_HEIGHT) {
          iterator.remove();
        }
      }
    }
    private void display() {
      // Clear screen
      System.out.print("\033[H\033[2J");
      System.out.flush();
      // Draw notes on screen
      char[][] screen = new char[SCREEN_HEIGHT][SCREEN_WIDTH];
      for (char[] row : screen) {
        Arrays.fill(row, ' ');
      }
      for (Note note : notes) {
        int x = note.getX();
        int y = note.getY();
        if (y >= 0 && y < SCREEN_HEIGHT && x >= 0 && x < SCREEN_WIDTH) {
          screen[y][x] = note.getSymbol();
        }
      }
      for (char[] row : screen) {
        for (char c : row) {
          System.out.print(c);
        }
```

```
        System.out.println();
      }
    }
    private void handleInput() {
      if (scanner.hasNextLine()) {
        String input = scanner.nextLine().toUpperCase();
        for (Note note : notes) {
          if (note.getY() == SCREEN_HEIGHT - 1 && input.length() == 1 && input.charAt(0)
== note.getSymbol()) {
            System.out.println("Hit!");
            notes.remove(note);
            break;
          }
        }
      }
    }
    public static void main(String[] args) {
      RhythmGame game = new RhythmGame();
      game.play();
    }
}
class Note {
    private int x;
    private int y;
    private char symbol;
    public Note(int x, char symbol) {
      this.x = x;
      this.y = 0; // Start at top of the screen
      this.symbol = symbol;
    }
    public int getX() {
      return x;
    }
```

```
    public int getY() {
        return y;
    }
    public void setY(int y) {
        this.y = y;
    }
    public char getSymbol() {
        return symbol;
    }
}
```

59. Color Matching Game

```
import java.util.*;
public class ColorMatchingGame {
   private static final String[] COLORS = { "RED", "GREEN", "BLUE", "YELLOW" };
   private static final Random random = new Random();
   private static final Scanner scanner = new Scanner(System.in);
   private int score = 0;
   private boolean gameOver = false;
   public void play() {
      System.out.println("Welcome to the Color Matching Game!");
      System.out.println("Match the color with the text.");
      while (!gameOver) {
         String colorText = COLORS[random.nextInt(COLORS.length)];
         String textColor = COLORS[random.nextInt(COLORS.length)];
         System.out.println("\nWhat color is the text: " + colorText + "?");
         System.out.println("1. RED");
         System.out.println("2. GREEN");
         System.out.println("3. BLUE");
         System.out.println("4. YELLOW");
         System.out.print("Enter your choice (1-4, or 0 to quit): ");
         int choice = scanner.nextInt();
         if (choice == 0) {
            gameOver = true;
            System.out.println("Game over. Final score: " + score);
         } else {
            String chosenColor = COLORS[choice - 1];
            if (chosenColor.equalsIgnoreCase(textColor)) {
               System.out.println("Correct! +" + scorePoint());
            } else {
               System.out.println("Incorrect! Game over. Final score: " + score);
               gameOver = true;
            }
         }
```

```
        }
        scanner.close();
    }
    private int scorePoint() {
        score++;
        return score;
    }
    public static void main(String[] args) {
        ColorMatchingGame game = new ColorMatchingGame();
        game.play();
    }
}
```

60. Simple Chatbot Game

```
import java.util.*;
public class SimpleChatbotGame {
    private static final String[] GREETINGS = { "Hello!", "Hi there!", "Hey!" };
    private static final String[] RESPONSES = {
        "That's interesting.",
        "Tell me more.",
        "I'm not sure about that.",
        "What do you think?",
        "Let's change the topic.",
        "Can you elaborate?",
        "Interesting point.",
        "I see. What else?"
    };
    private static final String[] TOPICS = {
        "technology",
        "movies",
        "food",
        "books",
        "travel"
    };
    private Random random = new Random();
    private Scanner scanner = new Scanner(System.in);
    public void startChat() {
        System.out.println("Welcome to the Simple Chatbot Game!");
        System.out.println("You can talk about various topics. Enter 'quit' to exit.");
        while (true) {
            System.out.print("\nEnter a message: ");
            String message = scanner.nextLine().toLowerCase();
            if (message.equals("quit")) {
                System.out.println("Goodbye!");
                break;
            }
```

```
        String response = generateResponse(message);
        System.out.println("Bot: " + response);
      }
      scanner.close();
    }
    private String generateResponse(String message) {
      if (isGreeting(message)) {
        return getRandom(GREETINGS);
      } else if (message.contains("technology")) {
        return "I love talking about technology!";
      } else if (message.contains("movies")) {
        return "What's your favorite movie?";
      } else if (message.contains("food")) {
        return "I'm hungry! Let's talk about food.";
      } else if (message.contains("books")) {
        return "Books are fascinating. Any recommendations?";
      } else if (message.contains("travel")) {
        return "I wish I could travel the world!";
      } else {
        return getRandom(RESPONSES);
      }
    }
    private boolean isGreeting(String message) {
      return message.contains("hello") || message.contains("hi") || message.contains("hey");
    }
    private String getRandom(String[] array) {
      return array[random.nextInt(array.length)];
    }
    public static void main(String[] args) {
      SimpleChatbotGame chatbot = new SimpleChatbotGame();
      chatbot.startChat();
    }
}
```

61. Bouncing Ball Animation

```
import javax.swing.*;
import java.awt.*;
import java.awt.event.ActionEvent;
import java.awt.event.ActionListener;
public class BouncingBallAnimation extends JPanel implements ActionListener {
  private static final int WINDOW_WIDTH = 800;
  private static final int WINDOW_HEIGHT = 600;
  private static final int BALL_SIZE = 50;
  private static final int BALL_SPEED = 5;
  private int ballX = 0;
  private int ballY = 0;
  private int ballXSpeed = BALL_SPEED;
  private int ballYSpeed = BALL_SPEED;
  public BouncingBallAnimation() {
    Timer timer = new Timer(1000 / 60, this); // 60 FPS
    timer.start();
  }
  public void paintComponent(Graphics g) {
    super.paintComponent(g);
    // Draw ball
    g.setColor(Color.RED);
    g.fillOval(ballX, ballY, BALL_SIZE, BALL_SIZE);
  }
  public void actionPerformed(ActionEvent e) {
    // Move ball
    ballX += ballXSpeed;
    ballY += ballYSpeed;
    // Check for collision with walls
    if (ballX <= 0 || ballX >= WINDOW_WIDTH - BALL_SIZE) {
      ballXSpeed = -ballXSpeed;
    }
    if (ballY <= 0 || ballY >= WINDOW_HEIGHT - BALL_SIZE) {
```

```
        ballYSpeed = -ballYSpeed;
      }
      // Repaint the panel
      repaint();
    }
    public static void main(String[] args) {
      JFrame frame = new JFrame("Bouncing Ball Animation");
      frame.setSize(WINDOW_WIDTH, WINDOW_HEIGHT);
      frame.setDefaultCloseOperation(JFrame.EXIT_ON_CLOSE);
      BouncingBallAnimation panel = new BouncingBallAnimation();
      frame.add(panel);
      frame.setVisible(true);
    }
}
```

62. Doodle Jump-style Game

```
import java.util.*;
public class DoodleJumpGame {
    private static final int PLATFORM_COUNT = 10;
    private static final int PLATFORM_WIDTH = 6;
    private static final int MAX_JUMP_HEIGHT = 3;
    private static final char PLAYER_CHAR = 'O';
    private static final char PLATFORM_CHAR = '-';
    private static final char EMPTY_CHAR = ' ';
    private int playerPosition;
    private List<Integer> platforms;
    private Random random = new Random();
    private Scanner scanner = new Scanner(System.in);
    public void play() {
        System.out.println("Welcome to Doodle Jump!");
        initializeGame();
        while (true) {
            displayGame();
            System.out.print("\nPress 'A' or 'D' to jump left or right (or 'Q' to quit): ");
            String input = scanner.nextLine().toUpperCase();
            if (input.equals("Q")) {
                System.out.println("Game over!");
                break;
            } else if (input.equals("A")) {
                movePlayer(-1); // Jump left
            } else if (input.equals("D")) {
                movePlayer(1); // Jump right
            }
            movePlatforms();
        }
        scanner.close();
    }
    private void initializeGame() {
```

```
    playerPosition = PLATFORM_COUNT / 2;
    platforms = new ArrayList<>();
    for (int i = 0; i < PLATFORM_COUNT; i++) {
      platforms.add(random.nextInt(PLATFORM_WIDTH));
    }
  }
  private void displayGame() {
    for (int i = 0; i < PLATFORM_COUNT; i++) {
      if (i == playerPosition) {
        System.out.print(PLAYER_CHAR);
      } else {
        int platformWidth = platforms.get(i);
        for (int j = 0; j < platformWidth; j++) {
          System.out.print(PLATFORM_CHAR);
        }
        for (int j = platformWidth; j < PLATFORM_WIDTH; j++) {
          System.out.print(EMPTY_CHAR);
        }
      }
      System.out.println();
    }
  }
  private void movePlayer(int direction) {
    playerPosition = Math.max(0, Math.min(playerPosition + direction, PLATFORM_COUNT
- 1));
  }
  private void movePlatforms() {
    for (int i = 0; i < PLATFORM_COUNT; i++) {
      if (random.nextDouble() < 0.2) {
        platforms.set(i, Math.max(0, Math.min(platforms.get(i) + random.nextInt(3) - 1,
PLATFORM_WIDTH - 1)));
      }
    }
```

```
    }
    public static void main(String[] args) {
        DoodleJumpGame game = new DoodleJumpGame();
        game.play();
    }
}
```

63. Reaction Time with Sound Effects

```
import javax.sound.sampled.*;
import java.io.File;
import java.io.IOException;
import java.util.Scanner;
public class ReactionTimeGame {
  private static final String SOUND_FILE_PATH = "path_to_your_sound_file.wav";
  public void play() {
    Scanner scanner = new Scanner(System.in);
    try {
      // Load sound file
      File soundFile = new File(SOUND_FILE_PATH);
      AudioInputStream audioInputStream = AudioSystem.getAudioInputStream(soundFile);
      Clip clip = AudioSystem.getClip();
      clip.open(audioInputStream);
      System.out.println("Get ready! Press Enter to start...");
      scanner.nextLine();
      // Play sound
      clip.start();
      // Measure reaction time
      long startTime = System.currentTimeMillis();
      System.out.println("Press Enter as soon as you hear the sound...");
      scanner.nextLine();
      long endTime = System.currentTimeMillis();
      long reactionTime = endTime - startTime;
      System.out.println("Your reaction time: " + reactionTime + " milliseconds");
      // Close resources
      clip.stop();
      clip.close();
      audioInputStream.close();
    } catch (UnsupportedAudioFileException | IOException | LineUnavailableException e) {
      System.out.println("Error: " + e.getMessage());
    } finally {
```

```
        scanner.close();

      }

    }

    public static void main(String[] args) {

      ReactionTimeGame game = new ReactionTimeGame();

      game.play();

    }

}
```

64. Puzzle Platformer

```
import java.util.*;
public class PuzzlePlatformer {
    private static final int LEVEL_COUNT = 3;
    private static final int MAX_MOVES_PER_LEVEL = 10;
    private int currentLevel;
    private int movesLeft;
    private Scanner scanner = new Scanner(System.in);
    public void play() {
        System.out.println("Welcome to the Puzzle Platformer Game!");
        for (currentLevel = 1; currentLevel <= LEVEL_COUNT; currentLevel++) {
            System.out.println("\n=== Level " + currentLevel + " ===");
            movesLeft = MAX_MOVES_PER_LEVEL;
            boolean completed = playLevel();
            if (completed) {
                System.out.println("Level " + currentLevel + " completed!");
            } else {
                System.out.println("Out of moves! Game over.");
                break;
            }
        }
        System.out.println("\nGame over! You completed " + (currentLevel - 1) + " levels.");
        scanner.close();
    }
    private boolean playLevel() {
        // Simulated level gameplay (puzzle solving)
        while (movesLeft > 0) {
            System.out.println("Moves left: " + movesLeft);
            System.out.println("Enter your move ('jump', 'move left', 'move right', 'use item'): ");
            String move = scanner.nextLine().toLowerCase();
            switch (move) {
                case "jump":
                    System.out.println("You jumped!");
```

```
                break;
            case "move left":
                System.out.println("You moved left.");
                break;
            case "move right":
                System.out.println("You moved right.");
                break;
            case "use item":
                System.out.println("You used an item.");
                break;
            default:
                System.out.println("Invalid move. Try again.");
                continue;
        }
        movesLeft--;
        // Simulate puzzle completion conditions (e.g., reaching the goal)
        if (random.nextInt(10) < 3) { // 30% chance of completing the level
            return true;
        }
    }
    return false;
  }
  public static void main(String[] args) {
    PuzzlePlatformer game = new PuzzlePlatformer();
    game.play();
  }
}
```

65. Balloon Pop Game

```
import java.util.*;
public class BalloonPopGame {
    private static final int GRID_SIZE = 5;
    private static final int MAX_MOVES = 10;
    private char[][] grid = new char[GRID_SIZE][GRID_SIZE];
    private int balloonsRemaining;
    private int movesLeft;
    private Scanner scanner = new Scanner(System.in);
    public void play() {
        System.out.println("Welcome to the Balloon Pop Game!");
        initializeGame();
        while (movesLeft > 0 && balloonsRemaining > 0) {
            displayGrid();
            System.out.println("Moves left: " + movesLeft);
            System.out.print("Enter the row and column (e.g., '3 4') to pop a balloon: ");
            int row = scanner.nextInt();
            int col = scanner.nextInt();
            if (isValidMove(row, col)) {
                if (grid[row][col] == 'O') {
                    grid[row][col] = 'X'; // Pop the balloon
                    balloonsRemaining--;
                    System.out.println("POP! Balloon popped at (" + row + ", " + col + ")");
                } else {
                    System.out.println("No balloon at (" + row + ", " + col + ")");
                }
                movesLeft--;
            } else {
                System.out.println("Invalid move. Try again.");
            }
        }
        displayGrid();
        if (balloonsRemaining == 0) {
```

```
            System.out.println("Congratulations! You popped all the balloons!");
        } else {
            System.out.println("Out of moves! Game over.");
        }
        scanner.close();
    }
    private void initializeGame() {
        balloonsRemaining = GRID_SIZE * GRID_SIZE;
        movesLeft = MAX_MOVES;
        // Initialize grid with balloons ('O')
        for (int i = 0; i < GRID_SIZE; i++) {
            for (int j = 0; j < GRID_SIZE; j++) {
                grid[i][j] = 'O';
            }
        }
    }
    private void displayGrid() {
        System.out.println("Current Grid:");
        for (int i = 0; i < GRID_SIZE; i++) {
            for (int j = 0; j < GRID_SIZE; j++) {
                System.out.print(grid[i][j] + " ");
            }
            System.out.println();
        }
    }
    private boolean isValidMove(int row, int col) {
        return row >= 0 && row < GRID_SIZE && col >= 0 && col < GRID_SIZE;
    }
    public static void main(String[] args) {
        BalloonPopGame game = new BalloonPopGame();
        game.play();
    }
}
```

66. Platformer with Double Jump

```
import java.util.*;
public class PlatformerWithDoubleJump {
    private static final int MAX_JUMPS = 2;
    private static final int MAX_HEIGHT = 10;
    private int playerPosition = 0;
    private int jumpsLeft = MAX_JUMPS;
    private Random random = new Random();
    private Scanner scanner = new Scanner(System.in);
    public void play() {
        System.out.println("Welcome to the Platformer with Double Jump!");
        while (playerPosition < MAX_HEIGHT) {
            displayGame();
            System.out.println("Jumps left: " + jumpsLeft);
            System.out.print("Press 'J' to jump (or 'Q' to quit): ");
            String input = scanner.nextLine().toUpperCase();
            if (input.equals("Q")) {
                System.out.println("Game over!");
                break;
            } else if (input.equals("J")) {
                if (jumpsLeft > 0) {
                    performJump();
                } else {
                    System.out.println("No more jumps left!");
                }
            }
        }
        scanner.close();
    }
    private void performJump() {
        playerPosition += random.nextInt(4) + 1; // Random jump height (1 to 4)
        System.out.println("Jumped to height: " + playerPosition);
        jumpsLeft--;
```

```
        if (jumpsLeft == 0) {
            System.out.println("No more jumps left!");
        }
    }
    private void displayGame() {
        System.out.println("Current Height: " + playerPosition);
    }
    public static void main(String[] args) {
        PlatformerWithDoubleJump game = new PlatformerWithDoubleJump();
        game.play();
    }
}
```

67. Galaga-style Shooter Game

```
import java.util.*;
public class GalagaShooterGame {
    private static final int PLAYER_STARTING_HP = 3;
    private static final int ENEMY_COUNT = 5;
    private static final int ENEMY_HP = 1;
    private static final int MAX_PLAYER_MOVES = 10;
    private int playerHP;
    private int playerPosition;
    private List<Integer> enemyPositions;
    private Random random = new Random();
    private Scanner scanner = new Scanner(System.in);
    public void play() {
        System.out.println("Welcome to Galaga Shooter Game!");
        initializeGame();
        while (playerHP > 0 && enemyPositions.size() > 0 && MAX_PLAYER_MOVES > 0) {
            displayGame();
            System.out.print("Enter the enemy position to shoot (1-" + enemyPositions.size() + "):
");
            int targetEnemyIndex = scanner.nextInt() - 1;
            if (isValidEnemyIndex(targetEnemyIndex)) {
                int targetEnemyPosition = enemyPositions.get(targetEnemyIndex);
                if (targetEnemyPosition == playerPosition) {
                    System.out.println("Player hit! Lose 1 HP.");
                    playerHP--;
                } else {
                    System.out.println("Enemy destroyed at position: " + targetEnemyPosition);
                    enemyPositions.remove(targetEnemyIndex);
                }
            } else {
                System.out.println("Invalid enemy position. Try again.");
            }
            MAX_PLAYER_MOVES--;
```

```
        }
        if (playerHP <= 0) {
            System.out.println("Game over! Player destroyed.");
        } else if (enemyPositions.size() == 0) {
            System.out.println("Congratulations! All enemies destroyed.");
        } else {
            System.out.println("Out of moves! Game over.");
        }
        scanner.close();
    }
    private void initializeGame() {
        playerHP = PLAYER_STARTING_HP;
        playerPosition = random.nextInt(ENEMY_COUNT) + 1; // Player starts at a random
position
        enemyPositions = new ArrayList<>();
        for (int i = 0; i < ENEMY_COUNT; i++) {
            enemyPositions.add(random.nextInt(ENEMY_COUNT) + 1); // Random enemy
positions
        }
    }
    private void displayGame() {
        System.out.println("Player HP: " + playerHP);
        System.out.println("Player position: " + playerPosition);
        System.out.println("Enemy positions: " + enemyPositions);
    }
    private boolean isValidEnemyIndex(int index) {
        return index >= 0 && index < enemyPositions.size();
    }
    public static void main(String[] args) {
        GalagaShooterGame game = new GalagaShooterGame();
        game.play();
    }
}
```

68. Card Sorting Game

```
import java.util.*;
public class CardSortingGame {
   private static final int DECK_SIZE = 5;
   private static final String[] SUITS = {"Hearts", "Diamonds", "Clubs", "Spades"};
   private static final String[] RANKS = {"2", "3", "4", "5", "6", "7", "8", "9", "10", "Jack",
"Queen", "King", "Ace"};
   private List<String> deck = new ArrayList<>();
   private Scanner scanner = new Scanner(System.in);
   public void play() {
      System.out.println("Welcome to the Card Sorting Game!");
      initializeDeck();
      shuffleDeck();
      System.out.println("Shuffled deck: " + deck);
      System.out.println("Sort the deck in order (e.g., 'Hearts 2', 'Clubs Ace'):");
      List<String> sortedDeck = new ArrayList<>();
      for (int i = 0; i < DECK_SIZE; i++) {
         System.out.print("Card " + (i + 1) + ": ");
         String input = scanner.nextLine();
         sortedDeck.add(input),
      }
      if (isSorted(sortedDeck)) {
         System.out.println("Congratulations! You sorted the deck correctly.");
      } else {
         System.out.println("Incorrect sorting. Better luck next time!");
      }
      scanner.close();
   }
   private void initializeDeck() {
      deck.clear();
      for (String suit : SUITS) {
         for (String rank : RANKS) {
```

```
                deck.add(suit + " " + rank);
            }
        }
    }
    private void shuffleDeck() {
        Collections.shuffle(deck);
    }
    private boolean isSorted(List<String> sortedDeck) {
        List<String> expectedDeck = new ArrayList<>(deck);
        Collections.sort(expectedDeck);
        return sortedDeck.equals(expectedDeck);
    }
    public static void main(String[] args) {
        CardSortingGame game = new CardSortingGame();
        game.play();
    }
}
```

69. Simple Soccer Game

```
import java.util.*;
public class SimpleSoccerGame {
    private static final int MAX_ROUNDS = 3;
    private static final int GOAL_THRESHOLD = 3;
    private String team1;
    private String team2;
    private int scoreTeam1;
    private int scoreTeam2;
    private Random random = new Random();
    private Scanner scanner = new Scanner(System.in);
    public void play() {
        System.out.println("Welcome to the Simple Soccer Game!");
        setupGame();
        for (int round = 1; round <= MAX_ROUNDS; round++) {
            System.out.println("\n--- Round " + round + " ---");
            playRound();
            displayScore();
        }
        displayWinner();
        scanner.close(),
    }
    private void setupGame() {
        System.out.print("Enter name for Team 1: ");
        team1 = scanner.nextLine();
        System.out.print("Enter name for Team 2: ");
        team2 = scanner.nextLine();
        scoreTeam1 = 0;
        scoreTeam2 = 0;
    }
    private void playRound() {
        // Simulate scoring goals in each round
        int goalsTeam1 = random.nextInt(GOAL_THRESHOLD + 1);
```

```
        int goalsTeam2 = random.nextInt(GOAL_THRESHOLD + 1);
        System.out.println(team1 + " scored " + goalsTeam1 + " goals!");
        System.out.println(team2 + " scored " + goalsTeam2 + " goals!");
        scoreTeam1 += goalsTeam1;
        scoreTeam2 += goalsTeam2;
    }
    private void displayScore() {
        System.out.println("Current Score:");
        System.out.println(team1 + ": " + scoreTeam1);
        System.out.println(team2 + ": " + scoreTeam2);
    }
    private void displayWinner() {
        System.out.println("\n--- Game Over ---");
        if (scoreTeam1 > scoreTeam2) {
            System.out.println(team1 + " wins!");
        } else if (scoreTeam2 > scoreTeam1) {
            System.out.println(team2 + " wins!");
        } else {
            System.out.println("It's a draw!");
        }
    }
    public static void main(String[] args) {
        SimpleSoccerGame game = new SimpleSoccerGame();
        game.play();
    }
}
```

70. Archery Shooting Game

```
import java.util.*;
public class ArcheryShootingGame {
    private static final int MAX_ARROWS = 5;
    private static final int MAX_SCORE = 50;
    private int totalScore = 0;
    private int arrowsLeft = MAX_ARROWS;
    private Random random = new Random();
    private Scanner scanner = new Scanner(System.in);
    public void play() {
        System.out.println("Welcome to the Archery Shooting Game!");
        while (arrowsLeft > 0 && totalScore < MAX_SCORE) {
            displayScore();
            System.out.print("Enter target distance (in meters): ");
            int distance = scanner.nextInt();
            int arrowScore = shootArrow(distance);
            totalScore += arrowScore;
            arrowsLeft--;
            System.out.println("You scored " + arrowScore + " points!\n");
        }
        displayFinalResult();
        scanner.close();
    }
    private int shootArrow(int distance) {
        int targetPosition = random.nextInt(distance) + 1; // Random target position within the
given distance
        int arrowPosition = random.nextInt(distance) + 1; // Random arrow position within the
given distance
        int distanceToTarget = Math.abs(targetPosition - arrowPosition);
        int arrowScore = calculateScore(distanceToTarget);
        return arrowScore;
    }
    private int calculateScore(int distanceToTarget) {
```

```
        if (distanceToTarget == 0) {
            return 10; // Bullseye
        } else if (distanceToTarget <= 5) {
            return 5; // Close to target
        } else if (distanceToTarget <= 10) {
            return 3; // Near target
        } else {
            return 0; // Missed target
        }
    }
    private void displayScore() {
        System.out.println("\nArrows left: " + arrowsLeft);
        System.out.println("Total score: " + totalScore);
    }
    private void displayFinalResult() {
        if (totalScore >= MAX_SCORE) {
            System.out.println("Congratulations! You reached the maximum score!");
        } else {
            System.out.println("Out of arrows! Game over.");
        }
        System.out.println("Final score: " + totalScore);
    }
    public static void main(String[] args) {
        ArcheryShootingGame game = new ArcheryShootingGame();
        game.play();
    }
}
```

71. Chess Timer

```
import java.util.Scanner;
public class ChessTimer {
    private static final int DEFAULT_TIME = 300; // Default time in seconds (5 minutes)
    private static final int TIME_INCREMENT = 10; // Time added per move in seconds
    private int player1Time;
    private int player2Time;
    private int currentPlayer;
    private Scanner scanner = new Scanner(System.in);
    public ChessTimer() {
        this.player1Time = DEFAULT_TIME;
        this.player2Time = DEFAULT_TIME;
        this.currentPlayer = 1; // Player 1 starts first
    }
    public void play() {
        System.out.println("Welcome to the Chess Timer!");
        while (player1Time > 0 && player2Time > 0) {
            displayTime();
            System.out.println("Player " + currentPlayer + ", enter your move (press 'Enter' to
confirm): ");
            scanner.nextLine(); // Wait for player's move
            updateTime();
            currentPlayer = (currentPlayer == 1) ? 2 : 1; // Switch turn to the other player
        }
        displayResult();
        scanner.close();
    }
    private void updateTime() {
        if (currentPlayer == 1) {
            player1Time -= TIME_INCREMENT;
        } else {
            player2Time -= TIME_INCREMENT;
        }
```

```
    }
    private void displayTime() {
        System.out.println("Player 1 Time: " + formatTime(player1Time));
        System.out.println("Player 2 Time: " + formatTime(player2Time));
    }
    private String formatTime(int seconds) {
        int minutes = seconds / 60;
        int remainingSeconds = seconds % 60;
        return String.format("%02d:%02d", minutes, remainingSeconds);
    }
    private void displayResult() {
        if (player1Time <= 0) {
            System.out.println("Player 2 wins! Player 1 ran out of time.");
        } else if (player2Time <= 0) {
            System.out.println("Player 1 wins! Player 2 ran out of time.");
        }
    }
    public static void main(String[] args) {
        ChessTimer timer = new ChessTimer();
        timer.play();
    }
}
```

72. Emoji Memory Match Game

```
import java.util.*;
public class EmojiMemoryMatchGame {
    private static final int BOARD_SIZE = 4; // Number of cards in each row/column
    private static final int TOTAL_PAIRS = BOARD_SIZE * BOARD_SIZE / 2; // Total pairs of
emojis
    private char[][] board = new char[BOARD_SIZE][BOARD_SIZE];
    private Set<Character> emojis = new HashSet<>();
    private Random random = new Random();
    private Scanner scanner = new Scanner(System.in);
    public void play() {
        System.out.println("Welcome to the Emoji Memory Match Game!");
        initializeGame();
        displayBoard();
        int matchedPairs = 0;
        while (matchedPairs < TOTAL_PAIRS) {
            System.out.println("\nEnter two coordinates (row1 col1 row2 col2) to reveal emojis
(e.g., 1 2 1 3): ");
            int row1 = scanner.nextInt() - 1;
            int col1 = scanner.nextInt() - 1;
            int row2 = scanner.nextInt() - 1;
            int col2 = scanner.nextInt() - 1;
            if (isValidInput(row1, col1, row2, col2)) {
                char emoji1 = board[row1][col1];
                char emoji2 = board[row2][col2];
                if (emoji1 == emoji2) {
                    System.out.println("Match found! Good job!");
                    board[row1][col1] = ' ';
                    board[row2][col2] = ' ';
                    matchedPairs++;
                } else {
                    System.out.println("No match. Try again.");
                }
```

```
            displayBoard();
        } else {
            System.out.println("Invalid input. Please try again.");
        }
    }
    System.out.println("\nCongratulations! You've matched all pairs. Game over!");
    scanner.close();
}
private void initializeGame() {
    List<Character> allEmojis = Arrays.asList('□', '□', '□', '□', '□', '□', '□', '□',
                                    '□', '□', '□', '□', '□', '□', '□', '□');
    emojis.addAll(allEmojis);
    // Fill the board with pairs of random emojis
    List<Character> shuffledEmojis = new ArrayList<>(emojis);
    Collections.shuffle(shuffledEmojis);
    Iterator<Character> iterator = shuffledEmojis.iterator();
    for (int i = 0; i < TOTAL_PAIRS; i++) {
        char emoji = iterator.next();
        placeEmojiOnBoard(emoji);
        placeEmojiOnBoard(emoji);
    }
}
private void placeEmojiOnBoard(char emoji) {
    while (true) {
        int row = random.nextInt(BOARD_SIZE);
        int col = random.nextInt(BOARD_SIZE);
        if (board[row][col] == '\u0000') {
            board[row][col] = emoji;
            break;
        }
    }
}
private void displayBoard() {
```

```
        System.out.println("\nCurrent Board:");
        for (char[] row : board) {
            for (char emoji : row) {
                System.out.print(emoji + " ");
            }
            System.out.println();
        }
    }
    private boolean isValidInput(int row1, int col1, int row2, int col2) {
        return row1 >= 0 && row1 < BOARD_SIZE && col1 >= 0 && col1 < BOARD_SIZE
&&
                row2 >= 0 && row2 < BOARD_SIZE && col2 >= 0 && col2 < BOARD_SIZE &&
                (row1 != row2 || col1 != col2) && board[row1][col1] != ' ' && board[row2][col2] != '
';
    }
    public static void main(String[] args) {
        EmojiMemoryMatchGame game = new EmojiMemoryMatchGame();
        game.play();
    }
}
```

73. Space Shooter Game

```
import java.util.*;
public class SpaceShooterGame {
    private static final int MAX_ENEMIES = 5;
    private static final int PLAYER_HEALTH = 3;
    private int playerHealth;
    private List<Integer> enemies = new ArrayList<>();
    private Random random = new Random();
    private Scanner scanner = new Scanner(System.in);
    public void play() {
        System.out.println("Welcome to the Space Shooter Game!");
        initializeGame();
        displayGameInfo();
        while (playerHealth > 0 && !enemies.isEmpty()) {
            System.out.print("\nEnter enemy ship ID to shoot (1-" + enemies.size() + "): ");
            int enemyIndex = scanner.nextInt() - 1;
            if (isValidEnemyIndex(enemyIndex)) {
                int enemyID = enemies.get(enemyIndex);
                System.out.println("You shoot down enemy ship " + enemyID + "!");
                enemies.remove(enemyIndex);
            } else {
                System.out.println("Invalid enemy ship ID. Please try again.");
            }
            displayGameInfo();
        }
        displayGameResult();
        scanner.close();
    }
    private void initializeGame() {
        playerHealth = PLAYER_HEALTH;
        for (int i = 1; i <= MAX_ENEMIES; i++) {
            enemies.add(i);
        }
```

```
        Collections.shuffle(enemies);
    }
    private void displayGameInfo() {
        System.out.println("\nPlayer Health: " + playerHealth);
        System.out.println("Remaining Enemies: " + enemies.size());
        System.out.println("Current Enemy Ships: " + enemies);
    }
    private boolean isValidEnemyIndex(int enemyIndex) {
        return enemyIndex >= 0 && enemyIndex < enemies.size();
    }
    private void displayGameResult() {
        if (playerHealth > 0) {
            System.out.println("\nCongratulations! You defeated all enemy ships!");
        } else {
            System.out.println("\nGame over! Your spaceship was destroyed by enemy ships.");
        }
    }
    public static void main(String[] args) {
        SpaceShooterGame game = new SpaceShooterGame();
        game.play();
    }
}
```

74. Sokoban Puzzle Game

```
import java.util.Scanner;
public class SokobanGame {
    private static final char WALL = '#';
    private static final char EMPTY = ' ';
    private static final char PLAYER = '@';
    private static final char BOX = '$';
    private static final char TARGET = '.';
    private static final char BOX_ON_TARGET = '*';
    private static final char PLAYER_ON_TARGET = '+';
    private char[][] grid;
    private int playerRow;
    private int playerCol;
    private int totalBoxes;
    private int boxesOnTargets;
    private Scanner scanner;
    public SokobanGame(char[][] grid) {
        this.grid = grid;
        this.scanner = new Scanner(System.in);
        initialize();
    }
    private void initialize() {
        totalBoxes = 0;
        boxesOnTargets = 0;
        for (int i = 0; i < grid.length; i++) {
            for (int j = 0; j < grid[0].length; j++) {
                if (grid[i][j] == PLAYER || grid[i][j] == PLAYER_ON_TARGET) {
                    playerRow = i;
                    playerCol = j;
                } else if (grid[i][j] == BOX) {
                    totalBoxes++;
                } else if (grid[i][j] == BOX_ON_TARGET) {
                    boxesOnTargets++;
```

```
            }
        }
    }
}
public void play() {
    System.out.println("Welcome to Sokoban!");
    while (true) {
        displayGrid();
        System.out.print("Enter your move (WASD or Q to quit): ");
        String move = scanner.nextLine().trim().toLowerCase();
        if (move.equals("q")) {
            System.out.println("Quitting the game...");
            break;
        }
        movePlayer(move);
        if (boxesOnTargets == totalBoxes) {
            System.out.println("Congratulations! You solved the puzzle!");
            break;
        }
    }
    scanner.close(),
}
private void movePlayer(String move) {
    int newRow = playerRow;
    int newCol = playerCol;
    switch (move) {
        case "w":
            newRow--;
            break;
        case "s":
            newRow++;
            break;
        case "a":
```

```
            newCol--;
            break;
        case "d":
            newCol++;
            break;
        default:
            System.out.println("Invalid move! Use WASD to move or Q to quit.");
            return;
    }
    char nextPos = grid[newRow][newCol];
    if (nextPos == EMPTY || nextPos == TARGET) {
        grid[playerRow][playerCol] = (grid[playerRow][playerCol] ==
PLAYER_ON_TARGET) ? TARGET : EMPTY;
        playerRow = newRow;
        playerCol = newCol;
        grid[playerRow][playerCol] = (nextPos == TARGET) ? PLAYER_ON_TARGET :
PLAYER;
    } else if (nextPos == BOX || nextPos == BOX_ON_TARGET) {
        int nextBoxRow = newRow + (newRow - playerRow);
        int nextBoxCol = newCol + (newCol - playerCol);
        char nextBoxPos = grid[nextBoxRow][nextBoxCol];
        if (nextBoxPos == EMPTY || nextBoxPos == TARGET) {
            grid[playerRow][playerCol] = (grid[playerRow][playerCol] ==
PLAYER_ON_TARGET) ? TARGET : EMPTY;
            playerRow = newRow;
            playerCol = newCol;
            grid[playerRow][playerCol] = (nextPos == BOX_ON_TARGET) ?
PLAYER_ON_TARGET : PLAYER;
            grid[newRow][newCol] = (nextBoxPos == TARGET) ? BOX_ON_TARGET : BOX;
            boxesOnTargets += (nextBoxPos == TARGET) ? 1 : 0;
            boxesOnTargets -= (nextPos == BOX_ON_TARGET) ? 1 : 0;
        }
    }
```

```
    }
    private void displayGrid() {
        for (char[] row : grid) {
            for (char cell : row) {
                System.out.print(cell);
            }
            System.out.println();
        }
    }
    public static void main(String[] args) {
        char[][] grid = {
            {'#', '#', '#', '#', '#', '#', '#', '#', '#', '#'},
            {'#', ' ', ' ', ' ', ' ', ' ', ' ', ' ', ' ', '#'},
            {'#', ' ', '.', '.', ' ', ' ', ' ', ' ', ' ', '#'},
            {'#', ' ', '.', ' ', ' ', ' ', ' ', ' ', ' ', '#'},
            {'#', ' ', '.', ' ', ' ', ' ', ' ', ' ', ' ', '#'},
            {'#', ' ', ' ', ' ', ' ', ' ', ' ', ' ', ' ', '#'},
            {'#', ' ', ' ', ' ', ' ', '$', ' ', ' ', ' ', '#'},
            {'#', ' ', ' ', ' ', ' ', ' ', ' ', ' ', ' ', '#'},
            {'#', ' ', ' ', ' ', ' ', ' ', ' ', ' ', ' ', '#'},
            {'#', '#', '#', '#', '#', '#', '#', '#', '#', '#'}
        };
        SokobanGame game = new SokobanGame(grid);
        game.play();
    }
}
```

75. Jungle Adventure Game

```
import java.util.Scanner;
public class JungleAdventureGame {
    private int playerHealth;
    private int distanceTraveled;
    private Scanner scanner;
    public JungleAdventureGame() {
        this.playerHealth = 10; // Initial player health
        this.distanceTraveled = 0; // Initial distance traveled
        this.scanner = new Scanner(System.in);
    }
    public void play() {
        System.out.println("Welcome to the Jungle Adventure Game!");
        while (playerHealth > 0) {
            System.out.println("\nCurrent Health: " + playerHealth);
            System.out.println("Distance Traveled: " + distanceTraveled + " km");
            System.out.print("\nEnter your choice (1 - Continue, 2 - Rest, 3 - Quit): ");
            int choice = scanner.nextInt();
            switch (choice) {
                case 1:
                    int distance = generateRandomDistance();
                    distanceTraveled += distance;
                    playerHealth -= distance / 2; // Health decreases as distance increases
                    System.out.println("You traveled " + distance + " km through the jungle.");
                    break;
                case 2:
                    playerHealth += 2; // Resting restores some health
                    System.out.println("You rested and recovered some health.");
                    break;
                case 3:
                    System.out.println("Exiting the game...");
                    scanner.close();
                    return;
```

```
            default:
                System.out.println("Invalid choice. Please try again.");
                break;
        }
        if (playerHealth <= 0) {
            System.out.println("Game over! Your health dropped to zero.");
            break;
        }
    }
    System.out.println("You survived the jungle adventure!");
    System.out.println("Final Distance Traveled: " + distanceTraveled + " km");
    scanner.close();
  }
  private int generateRandomDistance() {
    return (int) (Math.random() * 10) + 1; // Generate a random distance between 1 and 10 km
  }
  public static void main(String[] args) {
    JungleAdventureGame game = new JungleAdventureGame();
    game.play();
  }
}
```

www.ingramcontent.com/pod-product-compliance
Lightning Source LLC
Chambersburg PA
CBHW062136160726
48282CB00027B/842
* 9 7 8 9 3 3 4 0 5 0 1 9 6 *